EMPLOYEE ENGAGEMENT

A RECIPE TO BOOST ORGANISATIONAL PERFORMANCE

VIPUL SAXENA

INDIA • SINGAPORE • MALAYSIA

Notion Press

Old No. 38, New No. 6
McNichols Road, Chetpet
Chennai - 600 031

First Published by Notion Press 2019
Copyright © Vipul Saxena 2019
All Rights Reserved.

ISBN 978-1-68466-755-0

CONTENTS

Chandrakant (Dada) Patil
Minister
Revenue, Relief and Rehabilitation, Public Works (excluding Public Undertakings)
Government of Maharashtra

Date:- 06.03.2019

Congratulation for your first book titled "**Employee Engagement - A receipe to boost organisational performance**" which is ready to hit the stands in near future.

Writing a book is great service to the society in the form of "Thanks giving" for all that the society gave to all of us in past decades and I am sure that your book will not only be very useful to the industry but also to the students & academic community.

I wish that your book becomes a best seller.

C. B. Patil
(Chandrakant Patil)

Shri Dr. Vipul Saxena,
Mumbai.

Office : 302, Mantralaya (Annexe), Madam Kama Road, Mumbai - 400 032
✉ : cbpatil.minister@gmail.com ☎ +91 22 2202 4751 / 2202 5398

Dear Vipulji,

I am glad to note that your first book is being released on a very important topic **" Employee Engagement"** which is one of the key industrial challenge across globe and many Researches are underway to find a solution to enhance Employee Engagement Level.

I am more excited for this as you are not only able son of Kota and my College days friend too.

Please accept my heartiest congratulations on reaching one of most aspired miles stone by professionals of all domain.

Writing book is a great service to the society in the form of **"Thanks giving"** for all that the society gave to all of us in past decades.

I am confident that this Book, suitably titled **" Employee Engagement- A recipe to boost organisational performance"** will be able to guide not only HR Leaders, B School Students but also Research Scholars too.

Plesse accept my best wishes for the success of your Book making it Best Seller.

Warm Wishes

(Om Birla)

निवास : 80-ही, शक्ति नगर, कोटा, राजस्थान - 324009
14–विंडसर प्लेस, अशोका रोड, नई दिल्ली–110001
टेलीफैक्स : 0744-2505555, 011-23782409
सम्पर्क : 09783977701, 09414037200
e-mail : ombirlakota@gmail.com | website : www.ombirla.com

वस्त्र समिति

भारत सरकार, वस्त्र मंत्रालय

Textiles Committee

Government of India, Ministry of Textiles

P. Balu Road, Prabhadevi,
Mumbai - 400 025

Tel. :	+91-022-6652 7507 / 7510
Fax :	+91-022-6652 7509
Email :	secy.tc@nic.in
Website :	www.textilescommittee.gov.in

Ajit B. Chavan
Secretary

Dear Dr. Vipul Saxena,

I am glad to note that your first book is being released on a very important topic **"Employee Engagement – A recipe to boost organisational performance"** which is one of the key industrial challenge across globe and many Researches are underway to find a solution to enhance Employee Engagement Level.

I am confident that this Book, suitably titled "Employee Engagement - A recipe to boost organisational performance" will be able to guide not only HR Leaders, B School Students but Research Scholars as well.

I am sure that the solutions suggested in the book based upon your vast global experience in Human Resource Management functions in leading organisations, will be most pragmatic & applicable being developed through well researched data.

Please accept my best wishes for the success of your Book.

(Ajit B. Chavan)

Deepakkumar J. Mukadam

SENATE MEMBER
UNIVERSITY OF MUMBAI

Dear Vipul Saxena

I am glad to note that your first book is being released on a very important topic **"Employee Engagement"** which is one of the key industrial challenge across globe and many Researches are underway to find a solution to enhance Employee Engagement Level.

Writing book is a great service to the society in the form of **"Thanks giving"** for all that the society gave to all of us in past decades.

Please accept my heartiest congratulations on reaching one of most aspired miles stone by professionals of all domain.

I am sure your book will not only be very useful to the Industry but also to the students & academic community to understand real time connect between Employees Engagement & Organisational Performance along with other subsidiary factors as well.

I sincerely wish this book becomes a best seller.

Thanking You,

Deepakkumar Mukadam
Member, Board of Governors, IIM Jammu.
Chancellor's Nominee, University of Mumbai.

MOTI MAHAL, M. G. ROAD, GHATKOPAR (WEST), MUMBAI - 400 086. INDIA.
e-mail : mukadamdeepak@yahoo com • Tel. (O) : 2511 6538 • Fax : 2511 6598

Dr. Maqsood Ahmed Khan
MBA., Ph.D.
Chief Executive Officer

HAJ COMMITTEE OF INDIA
(Statutory body constituted under the Act of Parliament No.35 of 2002)
Ministry of Minority Affairs, Government of India.

Dear Dr Saxena,

I am glad to note that your first book is being released on a very important topic "**Employee Engagement**" which is one of the key industrial challenge across globe and many Researches are underway to find a solution to enhance Employee Engagement Level.

I am sure solution suggested in the Book by seasoned professional like you with vast global experience of spear heading Human Resource Management function in leading organisations,will be most pragmatic & applicable being developed through well researched data.

I am confident that this Book, suitably titled "Employee Engagement- A recipe to boost organisational performance" will be able to guide not only HR Leaders, B School Students but also Research Scholars too.

Pls accept my best wishes for the success of your Book.

Regards,

Dr. Maqsood Ahmed Khan
Chief Executive Officer
Haj Committee of India
Mumbai - 400 001.

Bidya S. Sahay <bssahay@gmail.com>
To: saxenavipui64@yahoo.com

28 Feb at 5:40 pm ★

Dear Dr Saxena,

I am glad to note that your first book is being released on a very important topic " Employee Engagement" which is one of the key industrial challenge across globe and many Researches are underway to find a solution to enhance Employee Engagement Level.

I am sure solution suggested in the Book by seasoned professional like you with vast global experience of spear heading Human Resource Management function in leading organisations,will be most pragmatic & applicable being developed through well researched data

I am confident that this Book, suitably titled " Employee Engagement- A recipe to boost organisational performance" will be able to guide not only HR Leaders, B School Students but also Research Scholars too.

Pls accept my best wishes for the success of your Book.

Thanks and regards,

BS Sahay
--

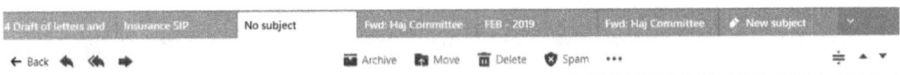

Prof. B.S. Sahay
Director
Indian Institute of Management Jammu
Old University Campus, Canal Road
Jammu (J&K) 180016
Mobile: +91 7000370470
E-mail: bssahay@gmail.com
Linkedin: https://www.linkedin.com/in/b-s-sahay-99298414/
Google Scholar: https://scholar.google.com/scholar?hl=en&q=%22BS+Sahay%22&oq=

Dear Dr. Vipul Saxena,

I am glad to know about your first book titled **"Employee Engagement- A recipe to boost organisational performance"** is ready to hit the stands in near future.

I am sure solution suggested in the Book by seasoned professional like you with vast global experience of spear heading Human Resource Management function in leading organisations, will be most pragmatic & applicable being developed through well researched data.

I am confident your book will not only be very useful to the Industry but also to the students & academic community to understand real time connect between Employees Engagement & Organizational Performance alongwith other subsidiary factors as well.

I sincerely wish this book becomes a best seller.

2 — 3 — 2019

DIRECTOR
Sydenham Institute of Management Studies
& Research & Entrepreneurship Education
'B' Road, Churchgate, Mumbai - 400 020.

संदीप शर्मा
विधायक
कोटा दक्षिण
राजस्थान विधानसभा, जयपुर

कार्यालय : 2—न—23, दादाबाड़ी,
कोटा—324 005 (राज.)
दूरभाष/फैक्स : 0744-2505556
मो. नं. : 94141-78500
E-mail : sandeepsharmabjp@gmail.com

क्रमांक :/४/*

दिनांक ०/२/२०१६

•Dear Vipul ji

This is the matter of proud and delight that your first book named "Employee Engagement' which is one of the key industrial challenge across globe and many researches are underway to find a solution to enhance Employee Engagement Level.

You make a name of not only your parents but also all India . The book will be boon for generations. Creation of a book means services of many generations. You are a part of readers .Creation and composing a book is like diven amrit which cofers immortality to both writer and reader.

The title of this book will prove its worthiness for young generation.

•My blessing and best wishes for the success of your book making it best seller.

With best complements.

(Sandeep Sharma)

R. Adm. (Retd) Vineet Bakhshi, VSM
Chief Executive
Govind Ram Memorial Educational Society

137, Shakti Nagar
Kota -324009 (Raj.)
Ph. : +91-744-2500196, 2500380
Mob. : 08058855888

Ex-CMD Goa Shipyard Ltd

Chairman QGO Finance Ltd

VB/01   05 Mar 19

Dear Mr Vipul Saxena,

It is a pleasure to see that you have written a research based
book on 'Employee Engagement', a nascent yet rapidly
developing concept in management theory and practice.

2. The pace of everyday life, rapidly changing societal
norms, a volatile social order, technologies and aspirations
in the twenty first century with facilities such as the
internet, which in many ways is a double edged sword too,
places special challenges on managements of all hues to
ensure that the employees are gainfully and increasingly
engaged, and, work with passion and commitment. The
book is therefore timely and can provide the lead for better
productivity and satisfied staff. The knowledge derived from
your research would undoubtedly assist industry and
management institutes to find ways and means to optimise
the potential of available human resources.

3. With best wishes

Yours Sincerely
Vineet Bakhshi

Mr Vipul Saxena

V. K. Jaitly
Sr. Vice President & Factory Head

(A UNIT OF DCM SHRIRAM INDUSTRIES LTD.)
SHRIRAM RAYONS
SHRIRAM NAGAR, KOTA (RAJ.) 324 004

March 09, 2019

Dear Vipul ji,

I am glad to note that your first book is being released on a very important topic " Employee Engagement" which is one of the key industrial challenge across globe and many Researches are underway to find a solution to enhance Employee Engagement Level.

I am more excited for this as you are an able son of Kota.

Please accept my heartiest congratulations on reaching one of most aspired miles stone by professionals of all domain.

Writing book is a form of 'thanks giving' to society, for all that we are taking from it during the journey of life.

I am confident that this Book, suitably titled "Employee Engagement- A recipe to boost organisational performance" will be able to guide not only HR Leaders, B School Students but also Research Scholars too.

Please accept my best wishes for the success of your Book making it Best Seller.

Best Wishes,

(V.K. JAITLY)

Mr. Vipul Saxena
Kota

OFFICE : TEL : (OFF.) 0744-2481519, 2481523, 2480001-4 Fax : 0744-2480003 Mobile : 9929590803 E-mail : vkjaitly@dcmsr.com
RESI. : 'KARUNA', E-213, SECTOR-E, SHRINATHPURAM, KOTA (RAJ.) TEL. : 0744-2471681-82

ACKNOWLEDGMENTS

Unlike other first time Authors my acknowledgement is lengthier (may appear my short auto biography) as I do come from Authors back ground and had very rich internship under my parents, mother being educationalist and father a Personnel Department Professional, English & Hindi Literature Writer. Additionally, It has always been my Gurus who saw potential in me and suggested & motivated me on right path that I have taken till date in past 50 yrs of my life.

I cannot begin without my gratitude to **my mother Late Mrs Vimla Saxena**, an English Lecturer by profession who channelized all my energies into right direction, be it academic or spiritual. She happened to be my first Guru in true sense channelizing my perceived intelligence to have much higher goals than my capabilities making me become Pilot and Engineer in Defence Forces. In making such career I had crossed many hurdles because of her emotional support. Simultaneously, she also enlightened spirituality in me at very early age and gave me **"Maa Gayatri" as Ista Devi**. Subsequently she introduced me to **my Guru Late Pt Badrinarayan Shastri**, MA (Sanskrit) a well blessed devotee of Devi who gave different & new dimension to my life in understanding and living life in a style mixed of spiritual cum practical. Under Guruji I practised & mastered many mantras procedurally and got inner self brightened up activating my chakras.

I am also grateful to **my father Late Shri Ramesh Chandra Saxena "Anil"** a multifariously talented being Freedom fighter, Politician, farmer, Poet/Author, Administrator and master in English & Hindi inherited to him from my **Grand father Late Shri Hanuman Prasad Saxena**, Freedom fighter, English teacher in British rule but promoted Hindi, established **"Bhartendu Samiti, Kota"** for upliftment of Hindi in backward state Rajasthan then, help the state join the mainstream politics of freedom movement filling the gap between regional language and Hindi. He too was well known Hindi Play Write Author of his time.

All my hard work and efforts to become Pilot in defence became reality only after getting blessings of **"Maa Gayatri"** under the guidance of Guruji. It was a dream come true for a boy like me who studied in Hindi Medium and physically very weak.

Blessings of **"Maa Gayatri"** was extended in all part of my life and continue till date, from my selection in Defence forces at SSB, Varanasi (UP) location very close to famous Temple of **"Maa Gayatri"** till marriage to Suvrita who belonged to **"Gayatri Parivar"** and was born at Varanasi, place where my career got kick start. She has always been with me in thick & thins of every part of my life.

Entry of our daughter **Kanika** was a precious moment in my life which gave me lot of strength and learning to maintain balance between career and family life, helping me take difficult decision to switch-over to Corporate Career to meet my responsibilities towards family after well dedicated & decorated defence career and start new career in much competitive & complex corporate world.

To meet challenges of corporate world, I have devoted lot of my personal time for learning new skills, techniques to keep pace with the world which could not have come through without sacrifices by my wife and daughter of their personal needs.

Even my Pet **"Cookie"(a Persian Cat)** is one who gave me company all through my journey of Phd during late/mid nights sitting next me. My Pets male & female Dog (Stray) Kuka & Kuki who gave me unconditional love to de-stress myself, helping me focus on Authoring this Book.

On professional front, I am highly indebted to **Dr RK Srivastava**, who was first one to see light in me and persuaded me for almost 3 years to undertake PhD and volunteered to be my guide. Without his motivation, guidance and support I would not have even started my PhD journey. He was one was always very helping and guided me on criticality of Research methodology and working on Thesis. Soon after my PhD, he was the main force who persuaded me to write Book on the Conceptual Model (Employee Engagement-Organisation Model) developed by me through my PhD Research.

Lastly, I would like to once again offer my sincere gratitude to all the personalities above for their continued support and blessings in completing this herculean task of my life which was again a dream come true at an age in life when people plan their retirement.

INDEBTED TO ALL & ALWAYS.

FROM AUTHOR'S DESK

Employee engagement is defined as involvement and commitment level that an employee exhibits towards their organization & its core values. It is a measure of employee's positive/negative attitude towards job, colleagues & organization which impacts their inclination to learn & execution at work.

Employee Engagement is linked to three vital goals of the organization: Productivity, Profitability & Attrition. Productivity is the key expectation of organisation from its employees. Engaged employee perform as per expectations of organisation and focus on performance & goal which assure & ensure success to the organization. Profitability is outcome of efforts of actively engaged manpower. Organisations always strive to hire/retain/develop committed, sincere & loyal employees who are capable of doing their jobs efficiently with absolute role & goal clarity.

Employee engagement has direct influence on productivity, loyalty, commitment levels and attrition. Organizations get all-round benefit from role played by loyal, committed, productive, and engaged employees.

The Book focuses on sharing & explaining research based study of employee engagement levels across various industries, ways to enhance employee engagement levels of an organisation and also understand relationship between employee engagement, employee well-being, organisation culture, employee satisfaction, employee performance, organization performance and attrition.

The Contents of the Book have been arrived at through analysis of Data collected by Survey Questioning 50 HR Heads, 600 White Collared Tech & non-Tech Employees and 600 Blue Collared Tech & non Tech Employees of 15 Industry spread across India.

The employee engagement survey data of existing employees of targeted industries was used to analyze and define employee engagement criteria. The analysis of Data also established connection between Employee engagement and organization culture and its impacts on Organizational performance in terms of productivity and profitability. It shows that more the employees are engaged more they are observed to be satisfied, loyal and use their full potential for completing the task linked to organisational goals.

Some of the crucial drivers/factors responsible for Employee Engagement are Salary (59%) leaves (83%), financial help for children education (67.5%), and medical facilities for self (76%), and medical facilities for family (71.5%) for both white collared and blue collared employees.

The Data also points to direct connection between employee engagement and organization culture and organization performance. The data analysis also established that employee engagement is crucial for job satisfaction, & employee loyalty and retention in the organization developing into a healthy organization culture which ultimately leads to better organization performance.

CHAPTER 1

INTRODUCTION

Every Organization strives for substantial growth each year. All the organizations who have achieved growth milestones much beyond planned are those with good and consistent track record of substantial Return on Investments and also well motivated teams.

Till late 80's, Industries never realised that Employees are backbone for Organizational growth. It was the entry of Multinational organisations in the Indian market which brought learning's to India Inc. that Human Resource is also as important contributor for an organizational performance as Financial capital and that the Human recourse too have key properties similar to Finance and therefore was started termed human work force as Human Capital/Human Equity.

In past two decades Industries globally have witnessed and earned huge returns by ensuring great care for Employee's concerns which enhanced motivation and retention of employees, as a result employee's performance played pivotal role in the growth of the organization as good as Business partners. This phenomenon has been termed as Employee engagement through Employee's well-being.

There have been many studies done by Organizations internally and also through Management consultants who have come out with useful data in terms of drivers & indicators to employee engagement and employee well-being.

Few Consultants have made progress towards linking employee engagement & employee well-being and its impact on organization performance.

Employee engagement was introduce to the industry about 2 decades ago as one of the possible tool for improving employee efficiency in any organisation. The momentum of this gained over past decade wherein most organisations considered employee engagement as one of the key organisational challenge & objective.

Despite popularity in service industry, Manufacturing industry was little late in adopting to the employee engagement. While the fact is that role of employees have day to day impact on the organisational performance and building up relationships among employees, peers, superiors and customer satisfaction etc.

While dealing with employee engagement of a particular industry, their specific needs are to be understood in terms of what factors would motivate and engage their employees. Each Industry segment has its peculiar concerns which are essentials to keep their employees motivated: upon these being addressed, employees feel engaged Creative people need good ambiance in the office, if that is provided they feel motivated and engaged etc.

Therefore purpose of this book is to establish factors effecting engagement of employees of Industry across, its current levels in similar organisations and ways to improve the engagement levels, thereby offering recipe to boost organisational performance. The Book has established the link between employee engagement, employee well-being, employee & organisational performance, organizational culture leading to casting a **"Conceptual Model"**

CHAPTER 2

QUANTITATIVE STUDY

SAMPLE SELECTION FOR THE BOOK

Considering such a complicated & vital challenge for Industry, a large size Sample was selected for the Research was as follows:

50 HR Heads of Manufacturing Industry were contacted.

600 White Coloured Tech & non Tech Employees of Manufacturing Industry were contacted and 600 Blue Coloured Tech & non Tech Employees of Manufacturing Industry were contacted.

IMPORTANT RESULTS AND DISCUSSION

The Study collected and analysed data of existing Employee engagement levels in manufacturing industries and how to improve the same. The Study will help HR Heads to design appropriate Employee engagement policies which can be customised to meet their retention the talent pool.

The Study collected and analysed data of existing employees Well-being levels in manufacturing industries to define Well-being criteria and How each criteria is affected by employee engagement levels of the organization. This will help HR Heads to measure impacts of Employee Engagement Policies on the Employee Well-being.

The Study Tested the Hypothesis of the Objectives to establish direct relation between employee engagement and well-being and its linkage to organization Performance. The Study will help HR Heads to make necessary amendments/additions/ deletions to Employee Engagement Policies where necessary to improve organizational performance in terms of productivity and profitability.

Using Analysis of data collected the Study was conducted to Develop Measurement techniques of Wellbeing of employees and Design a Model which co-relates Wellbeing and Employee Engagement rationally. This will help HR Heads mapping existing Employee Well-being levels; define next levels which helps enhance employee contribution in achieving Organization goals in terms of productivity and profitability.

DATA COLLECTION AND ANALYSIS

Employees	Gender		Mean Age	Mean experience	Total
	Male	Female			
HR head/ Managers	30	20	–	–	50
White collared employees	390	210	26–35 yrs	2–3 yrs	600
Blue collared employees	366	234	26–35 yrs	6–10 yrs	600
Total	786	464			1250

DEMOGRAPHICS OF DATA ANALYSIS

To conduct detailed study of the objectives & assumptions among employees working under varied professional, social, financial setup, survey was conducted in various manufacturing organizations in different product & process segments. Three categories of employees e.g. Blue coloured, White coloured and HR Managers were selected for the survey from different Organizations in manufacturing industry. The objective of these 03 category of employees was considered so as to get response from worker class, executives class can be taken on the effects of organisation's engagement initiatives and decision to include HR managers for survey response was taken as to study how effective HR policies were and what they feel the bottlenecks in employee engagement.

As employees are the asset of the manufacturing industry, and the vital part of the performance in terms of productivity and profitability of the Organization depends upon the blue coloured employees to great extent. Then it comes the White collared employees who help Organization to manage different departments like finance, marketing, HR and technical. These executives are second most important asset of the Organization. Then the HR department and the HR managers who help Organization by making policies suitable and beneficial to the employees and looking after their basic needs to get fulfilled. The HR manager too has a vital role in Organization performance, as he/she has to make such HR policies which are beneficial to both Organizations as well as employees and to make employee happy, satisfied and so engaged at the workplace.

50 HR Managers were interviewed personally/telephonically and were asked to respond to questionnaire to study the impact of HR policies of different Organization on employee engagement objectives of the organisation. 600 white collared employees and 600 blue collared employees were interviewed in person/ telephonically, told to fill the questionnaire in person and online

to study how effective the employee engagement policies of their organisations are and what else the employees expect from the management. As priority and quantum of needs of employees were considered to be varying among different categories both blue and white coloured employees were included in the study to respond the questionnaire.

EMPLOYEES INVOLVED IN SURVEY

Employees	Gender	Frequency	Percentage
Blue collared	Male	366	29.00
	Female	234	19.00
White collared	Male	390	31.00
	Female	210	17.00
HR Managers	Male	30	2.00
	Female	20	2.00
Total		1250	100.00

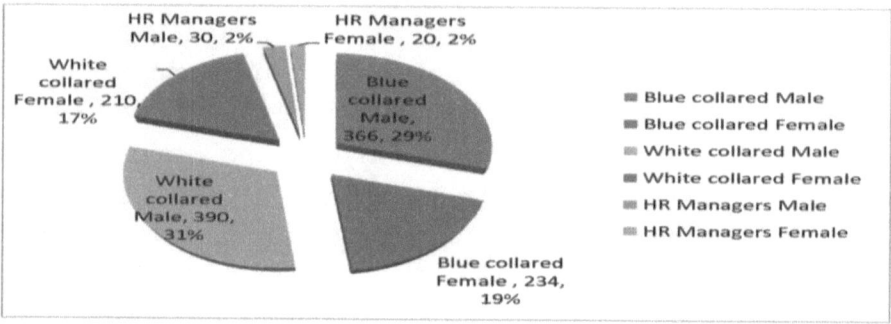

EMPLOYEES INVOLVED IN SURVEY

Out of 600 blue collared employees 366 were male and 234 were females. The male: female ratio is 61:31. While for white collared employees, 390 males and 210 females participated in the survey ranging from 21 yrs to 55 yrs of age group. The mean age for both the employees is 26 to 35 years. The male –female ratios forms fairly well represented sample of the population.

The mean experience for white collared employees in the Organization is 2 years to 3 years while for blue collared employees it is 6 years to 10 years. White collared employees/ executives and managers tend to switch their job frequently i.e.

in 2 to 3 years while most of the stick to one Organization i.e. more than 4 yrs which is 32% of all employees. This indicates that they were loyal to Organization which is because of so many reasons like job satisfaction, employee engagement and other policies which are in benefit of employees.

Out of 600 employees nearly 290 employees i.e. 46.5% employees had prior experience. The mean age of experience is 2.66 and the median year of experience is 3 years.

CHAPTER 3

ASSUMPTIONS BASED ON QUALITATIVE RESEARCH

Researches in the area of employee engagement and well-being of employees in emerging market like India and how to measure it and its impact were conducted by very few researchers, and the studies too were done in piece meal fashion. This is very important for sustained growth in Manufacturing sector, needs of one of the key assets of the organization i.e. Employee's- to be taken care of. When they are taken care well, it improves their well-being and satisfaction levels, resultantly employees will be more productive & loyal and will play pivotal role in achieving the goals of organization.

The Global Markets have become too competitive due to advancement of technologies and also profit margin shrinking. Role played by employee have become highly specific & specialized and thereby have become major variable for cost control. Hence, Industry has apparently accepted the value of Human Capital, and they are faced with challenge of attracting new talent, grooming & retention of existing talents.

Attracting, developing and retaining the right Talent, Employee engagement is new age challenge for the HR Managers in the industry. Developing employees is a scientific & procedural activity but engagement has yet not become as scientific which can directly relate to particular HR initiative as engagement is resultant of HR initiative and its impact on cognitive/emotional level of the employee.

Well-being till now has been a generalized term as the Industry is still not sure the parameters which actually define and relate to well-being. Well-being is directly related to employee engagement but the Industry also not sure which Employee engagement policy is essential and what will be its contribution to employee engagement matrix in achieving organizational goal.

As Employee engagement and well-being have become one of the key challenge/activity which need to be managed to achieve organization goal, there is need to map and measure these and also establish the link between these with organizational performance.

The relationship between employee well-being and employee engagement is not studied in the Indian context in manufacturing industry yet. The relationship is presumably direct and it impacts the organization performance. So there is a need for a detailed study of these parameters to measure the well-being and employee engagement criteria and how it affects the employee satisfaction, employee loyalty, improve attrition rate and enhance performance of employees and the organization.

Assumptions about link among Employee Engagement, Employee Wellbeing, Employee Performance and Organisation Performance

World over Industry has accepted that Human Resource is as Asset for an Organization and play vital role in Organizational performance, in terms of productivity and profitability, towards achieving its strategic goals of expansion and growth.

Over the years Industry has unanimously reached a conclusion that Human Resource is not a Cost head but an asset. Further, it has also been well accepted that cost involved in developing and retaining the human resource is an investment than expenditure as the Organization gets the ROI on human resource development and retention in multiples to the expenditures incurred on this initiative. Hence, Attrition of human resource has become a big challenge for the HR leaders globally and one of the major KRA of their own performance matrix.

Therefore, HR leaders work day-night to conduct various surveys and study developmental needs and reasons for attrition and keep designing various policies to retain the well trained human resource.

In the above pursuits the HR leaders across the globe have arrived at a conclusion that two variables' namely Employee Engagement and Employee Well-being are the solution to manage the Attrition.

Despite tire less efforts by HR leaders across the globe, to design and implement employee engagement and well-being policies they have yet not been able to establish measurable link between Employee Well-being and Employee Engagement.

There have been numerous studies carried out by HR professional and HR Consulting organisations, through which they have been able to establish Employee Well-being and Employee engagement as two variables directly linked to third variable i.e. organizational performance. But there is no measurement process or tool designed yet which can establish quantitative relationship between Employee Well-being and Employee Engagement and its impact on organisation performance in terms of productivity and profitability.

The book furnishes meaningful investigation in understanding inter-relationship between Employee Well-being and Employee Engagement and a measuring model for the same and its impact on organisation performance in terms of productivity and profitably.

Assumption 1 (H1): Employee Engagement is not affected significantly by Employee Well being.

Once employee engagement triggers employee well-being, it triggers the employee engagement to next level and leads to a cycle of well-being through employee engagement; observing benefits of employee well-being, some of the employees out of employee who are not yet engaged get motivated & result in enhanced employee engagement level in the organisation to some extent but not significantly.

Assumption 2 (H2): Employee Engagement significantly affect Employee Performance.

Employee engagement policies of the organization make employee feel that the organization cares for his/her concerns about personal welfare and congenial work environment which results into developing feeling of well-being making him/her belong to the organization termed as loyalty. This emotional relationship between employee and organization improve retention through reduced attrition and enhances employee performance in terms of productivity resulting into improved organization performance in terms of productivity & profitability.

Assumption 3 (H3): There is not any significant effect of Employee Engagement on Organisation Performance.

Employee engagement initiatives are aimed at improving organization culture in terms of welfare of employees and congenial work place. These initiatives makes employees feel that organization is concerned about his/her personal welfare and also quality of work environment in terms of clarity in role & responsibility, transparent & socially neutral performance evaluation process, office equipments etc.

These initiatives induce well-being feeling among employees. Once the feeling of well-being sets in among the employees it shows its impacts on a larger scale in terms of number, grades of employees resulting feeling of well-being across the board.

Employee engagement triggers feeling of well-being among employees, with the passage of time and continuity of engagement policies feeling of well-being though restrictively but improves employee engagement among the employees this sets in a cycle of well-being through engagement and restrictive enhanced engagement through well-being. This cycle of engagement and well-being induces loyalty among employees towards the organization

Improved employee well-being induces loyalty in the employee towards his/her organization and at some level he/she even becomes Organization Brand ambassador among the employees, especially among new joinees. Organizations using Buddy System to engage new joinees at faster pace often use employee with scores of well-being. Well-being motivates employee's dedication and devotion to the role assigned which improves his/her performance as team member & team leader resulting in improved organizational performance though not significantly.

CHAPTER 4

TALENT MANAGEMENT & EMPLOYEE ENGAGEMENT

4.1. IMPORTANCE OF HUMAN RESOURCE/EMPLOYEES IN THE ORGANIZATION

Human resource is the most important resource for any organization as all the major functions are highly dependants upon the employees of the organization. It is the efficient manpower that is identity of an organisation which proves that manpower is of vital importance for an organisation. Meeting this task is termed as Talent acquisition/management function. This function starts a cycle from Recruitment of Right person for the Right job at Right time with Right attitude. Once hired, the management is responsible to deploy these employees suitably. Corporate HR is expected to prepare manpower planning, before recruitment so that head counts and manpower cost is kept under control and yet organisation is able to achieve the targets utilising man power appropriately.

4.2. MANUFACTURING INDUSTRY IN INDIA

The term Manufacturing is used for converting raw material into consumable/usable/finished goods/inter mediate to finished goods using machine, manual process/technical process/ chemical process whether it is manufacturing of eatables, equipment, cosmetics, vehicles, even aircraft etc. These products are sold to the whole sellers/distributors who in turn sell this to retailers which ultimately reach end consumers.

Manufacturing activity plays key role in GDP of most countries especially India. Manufacturing activities are undertaken for higher volumes of production so that larger quantities are produced at lower cost. Subsequently, after staking for domestic consumption surplus quantities are exported to other countries which generate foreign currency funds which are used for imports of critical/essential supplies for public consumption/ defence equipments etc.

Under free economies manufacturing activities are done for planned quantities as per state determined central plans while for mixed economies its done under state controlled regulations.

Many researchers have predicted that there are huge increases in domestic consumption in India and many MNCs are looking upto India as manufacturing hub due to abundant resources and cheaper man-power which will take Indian manufacturing sector to $ 1 Trillion by 2025.

This growth prospects have motivated domestic and global manufacturers due to great opportunities to invest in India which in turn will enhance contribution of manufacturing sector in GDP from 13–16% to 25–30% and generating 100 million approx. jobs in India by 2025.

Growth Trend

HSBC PMI (purchase manager's index) generated as per reply by purchase managers of 500 organisations to questionnaire PMI counts were 52 in March 2013, 51.4 in Jan 2014 and 52.5 in Feb 2014 which incredibly high on y-o-y and encouraging as score 50 and above is considered sustained growth.

FMCG and basic consumer goods sector were observed to be best performing and substantial growth pace due to increase in out puts and consumer behaviours in India and also increase in exports as Indian products now can compete in global market due to meeting global quality standards.

Manufacturing: Government Initiatives

While addressing World Economic Forum (WEF), Indian Commerce Minister in 2014, informed the forum that India would create 05 National Investment and Manufacturing Zones (NIMZs) outside DMIC region at Nagpur (Maharashtra), Tumkur (Karnataka), Chittoor, Medak and Prakasam (Andhra Pradesh) for manufacturing sector. This would create about 100 million jobs by 2025 and increase contribution of manufacturing sector to Indian GDP from 13–16% to 20–25%. However, he insisted that t bring this dream come true India industry will have to accelerate its Exports and put onus on State Govts to acquire necessary land pool for these infrastructure developments.

Road Ahead

As Govt of India has realised that it is manufacturing sector which need to boost if Indian Economy has to be grown faster and sustained and for that many reform in Labour policy, Land acquisition, FDI, Licensing system etc are to be on top priority. Another development which will help economic growth is Policy & incentives on Exports of finished goods.

India's exports have grown from US$ 8.1 BN in 2007 to US$ 20.9 BN by 2011, which is a very significant indicator of growth prospect of Indian manufacturing Industry. Out of the whole kitty of exports from India Hitech Exports has recorded Compound Annual Growth Rate (CAGR) of 26% in 2007–11. Electronic goods and Pharma too have grown substantially over past 10 years. These trends show a very rosy picture for India Manufacturing Industry and Exports.

4.3. TALENT MANAGEMENT AS CRITICAL AS CAPITAL MANAGEMENT

It is a key HR function consisting of Planning, hiring, developing, and retaining the talent in any organisation to ensure that the required talent pool is available to sustain the existing business, grow the business, strategic business decisions e.g Joint ventures, merger & acquisitions, setting new SBU.

In pre 1950 Era, organisations used to consider and treat talent as "worker/servant" and work culture was restricted to obey the order given by the promoter/manager. With the industrial globalisation and consumerism becoming the realty of business scenario, same worker/servant transformed into talent and been accepted as key role player in business form &performance at any stage of business.

In the present day organisations have ful-fledged and well geared up HR department which is tasked with Talent management. Talent management is one of the key KRA of HR teams in the organisations. HR teams are tasked with hiring goals with strict time lines and also keeping attrition within control limits.

4.3.1 Need for Talent Management: strategic perspectives

As global market becoming cut throat competitive the Industry has realised importance of acquiring and retaining talent best suited for its business goals. In the recent decades, Industry has started including Manpower factors in all its strategic capital investment decisions such as JV venture, Mergers & Acquisitions and setting up new SBU.

The Industry has escalated their HR department more aggressively geared up for understanding & undertaking Manpower due diligence and acquisition and retention to meet newer business challenges. In order to undertake such tasks HR departments are led by strong & seasoned HR leader with astute strategic bent of mind, and HR departments have exclusive Talent Management team. These Talent management teams have their goals aligned with capital investment goals.

The Talent management teams are given hiring targets and retention targets to ensure that any given time organisation is manned by desired skilled manpower to meet the organisational challenges and goals.

The HR leaders have their eyes on Talent need targets as critical goals for their teams. In meeting such targets the HR leaders regularly interact with business leaders and top management to cast their Talent planning & strategies aligned with the business goals. Such exercise is undertaken and concluded by Oct-Dec of each year keeping enough open room to re align with the changing needs of business goals due to various variable factors turning unfavourable/hostile.

Though from the very first step, every business venture need talent management to achieve financial goals & growth but as at the inception stage most start-ups management have other business challenges as their priorities than man power management without realising it one of the key need for the business success.

However growing organisations do understand this need and include Talent management as one of their key strategic goals for success &growth.

Following are key strategic perspective for talent management:

a. Process orientation

Most Organisations have well realised that days of person driven organisation are over, now the market is so competitive that need every business activity to be undertaken by employee with specific competencies for the role. All the business processes strictly demand suitably qualified talent armed with required behavioural competency for the role.

b. Cultural need

This perspective suggests that every organisation has its work culture customised to the management style and market challenges. Hence, most organisations in addition to technical skills and behaviroal competency also look for attitude as team member and team leader.

c. Competitive edge

In fierce competitive market, one of the key challenges faced by the Organisations is continuous flow of talent pool to meet the growth plan and also market needs. Hence, organisations through its Talent management group hire, develop and retain sufficient talent for current, future and contingent competitive needs of the market.

d. Human Resource Planning perspective

Most organisations over the period have realised the importance of man power planning for two fold objective;

1. To have sufficient talent availability at all times;
2. To have right person for the right job with right attitude. This process ensure continuous supply of desired human resource.

e. Change management need perspective

As organisation grows, at every new level it attains unless there is a continuous process of developing the existing manpower or inducting fresh talent in the system, big lot of existing man power becomes redundant due to pace gap.

Hence, to meet the newer challenges organisation goes through "Change management process" which need lateral induction of new leaders and also developing potential employees as leaders.

4.3.2 Drivers for Talent Management

Based on various perspective discussed above following factors are identified as Drivers for Talent Management:

a. Attracting new Talent
b. Hiring Talent
c. Apt Deployment of existing & new Talent
d. Developing existing & new Talent
e. Re-appropriation of existing talent
f. Rationalisation of Talent pool
g. Motivating Talent pool: Job satisfaction, Appropriate Compensation & benefits
h. Engaging Talent pool
i. Managing redundant Talent
j. Maintaining controlled & healthy attrition
k. Retaining desired Talent
l. Succession planning

4.3.3 Employee engagement a key to Talent Management

Roller – coaster journey of global Industrial development saw changing scenario of management perspective and accordingly change in Management strategy which began from Customer Satisfaction as key to Business success where only "Quality" of product/service as Customer satisfaction to Customer satisfaction in terms of quality, post-sale services, value added services and lastly as Customer delight.

Later management perspective found newer shape transiting from Customer Satisfaction to Employee Engagement where in Employee satisfaction in terms of job satisfaction, growth opportunity, financial growth & Employee motivation etc been main constituents as key to Business success. Thus, in the current business scenario Industrial growth journey reached a level where Industry accepted that managing Human capital is as costly & critical for Business success as decision and process of Capital investment and need great care in handling as it has direct impact on the employee performance, which ultimately affect organisational performance.

4.3.4 Talent management Best Practices

Considering current business challenges at global level, Talent management has become very critical & costly function for almost all the ambitious Organisations and accordingly they have included Talent management in key priority strategic decisions and included HR leaders as team member of Business Strategic Group of the Organisation.

As most of the Talent Management Strategies focus on balancing Organisational talent needs and need for engaged, satisfied and motivated lot of desired talent pool, following Talent management strategies can be universally applicable:

a. Recruitment & Induction Practices
b. Supportive Top Management Team
c. Talent Evaluation & Succession Planning Practices
d. Performance Management Practices
e. Compensation & Benefit Practices
f. Organisational Leadership Development Culture
g. Role based customised Leadership Development practices
h. Talent management ROI analysis Practices

4.3.5. Literature Review

Frynas, Millahi & Pigman.(2006); Karim, (2006); Barsade & Donald, (2007) suggested that Business ventures and organizations should evolve their own pool of talent as per their growing needs to match demanding global business environment.

Arporn (2008) opined organisations must grow their human capital stock as per the global needs, in terms of improving their performance and working style.

Schon & Ian, (2009) stated in their publication "The global war for talent" that global changes in market scenario has induced demand and competition in acquiring & retaining talent globally and advised talent management as challenging goal of organizational development.

Richard et. al. (2011) alerted the organisations about immediate need of talent management challenges and need of strong and robust Human Resource for success of an organization.

(Inkson, 2008 & Rousseau, 2001) referred a shift in the power relationship between employers and employees and that gradually, organizations are accepting consumerist a key reason for talent management a new business challenge.

(Huang & Tansley, 2012)stated that majority of publications on talent management do not offer a formal definition of the central concept.

(Lewis & Heckman, 2006) not many organizations have a talent management system in place.

Iles, Preece, & Chuai, 2010; Tansley, 2011) unanimously summed up that talent management add value over all the HRM strategies & practices.

Ashton & Morton (2009) Talent management includes managing demand & supply and continuous flow of talent in an organisation.

Over the years due to changed business scenario globally, Talent management has evolved as key business strategic decision & functions as it has been proved that it is the satisfied, engaged, motivated talent pool which directly impacts Organisational performance.

Talent management includes activities/initiatives to Attracting, Inducting, Deploying, Developing, Assessing, Engaging, Satisfying, Motivating existing and new talent pool.

Out of the key talent management strategies Employee Engagement plays vital role in ensuring the desired talent at any time & continuous flow of talent focusing on their performance aligned to organisational goals.

All ambitious organisations across the world have made sustained efforts to develop vibrant HR department to ensure a vibrant organisation armed with engaged, satisfied & motivated Talent rich with desired technical and behavioural competencies, apt attitude and potential for development & career growth.

As employee performance directly impacts organisational performance; Talent management is considered as costly &critical investment as Capital investment for any organisation.

4.4 ENGAGED ORGANISATIONS & EMPLOYEE ENGAGEMENT

Engaged organisations work on strong value based practices with visible link between employee & employers mutual faith and natural justice, as mutual promise & commitment between employer and employee is essential ingredient as an understanding & fulfilment.

Though improvement in productivity thereby enhanced performance is at the epicentre of engagement, however it cannot be extracted by any mechanism of wilful manipulation of employees' commitment and emotions.

These days Employees too are well aware of various manipulating tactics of management hence they are able to quickly pin point such attempts; which lead instead to cynicism and disillusionment. While employees already at engaged state voluntarily give desired effort, as an integral essence of their duty at work.

Employee engagement is not repackaged old management styles but have connections with analytical factors e.g. commitment, job involvement, organisational behaviour & job satisfaction, apart from few critical differences.

Employee engagement is an interdependent mechanism based on trust and under-standing: organisations must endeavour to engage employees, and in turn offer credible engagement scores to management. It mutually emphasizes each other. Employee engagement is medium of driving employee well-being and thereby enhancing their performance. Data of various research and survey indicates engaged organisation's productivity enhances by 43% and overall performance by 20%. Such organisation's retention improves by 87%.

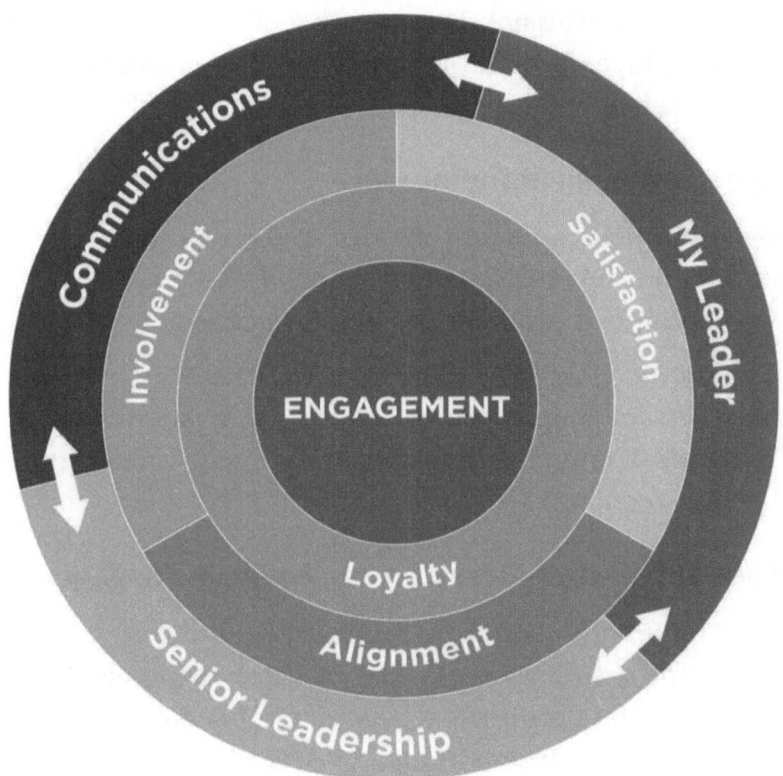

Figure 1: Employee engagement

4.4.1 Employee engagement

Employee Engagement is a developing incidence in the Industry that is ensured by HR leaders and also by Line managers. In the present Business Scenario the managers of every level are always keen to identify whether employees in his team are engaged or disengaged?

As dis-engagement/mis-alignment is one of the most probable reasons for employees losing commitment & motivation levels, a disrespectable work generally causes detachment &apathy from job role & organisation.

Such employees are considered as alienated from their job roles. Many researchers have connected engagement through involvement & enthusiasm to results of engagement such as attrition, employee productivity, profitability & safety, customer delight & loyalty.

Employee Engagement Definitions

Employee happiness doesnt mean Employee Engagement, this should also not be construed as employee will work extra hard and with enhanced productivity help organisation grow.

Recreational facilities provided by the Organisation are definitely attract employees to distress and keep them fit but their gestures of enjoying these facilities doesn't mean that those employees are engaged.

Employee satisfaction doesn't mean Employee engagement

Most organisations conduct "employee satisfaction" surveys each year and employees do give positive response indicating "employee satisfaction", but it has been observed that satisfied employee may be happy enough to attend office regularly but may not be willing to put extra hard work which means that such employee are satisfied but not engaged.

Employee engagement indicates emotional commitment with the Organisation which points to the fact that such employees are concerned about survival & growth of their organisation and also committed to organisational goal. Such employees work for organization's goals than just for their pay cheque and career growth.

Employee engagement is point of intersection between maximum contribution for the business and maximum satisfaction for employees. It is termed as sustainable level of high performance which is beneficial to both the Organisation and the employee.

Engagement is broadly connected to key objectives of all the organizations. Engaged employees ensure enhanced productivity to such an extent that it improves profitability of an organisation. Such objectives are achieved when employees are clear about their job roles and have trust on management which turn get them engaged and improve retention levels of an organisation (The Essentials of Employee Engagement in Organizations Author: Simon, Simeon S2011)

Authors (Shuck and Authors Wollard, 2010,) have quoted Employee engagement as "Employee's emotional, cognitive & behavioural attitude that play vital role for targeted organizational results".

(Saks, 2006) (Wagner and Harter, 2006; Kahn, 1990) referred that "Engaged Employees are always found to be alert & fully involved in job role emotionally and mentally for their role in the organisation.

Researcher States (2008) advocated that most organisations are focussing on employee engagement and investing on resources for developing employee engagement.

(Macey and Schneider, 2008; Macey et al., 2009) stated that Organisations believe that employee engagement is a key initiative to take on market competition and also mitigate organisational challenges.

Research studies have indicated that organizations with better employee engagement echelons reap most of the organisational gaols in terms of performance and financial indicators (Kular et al., 2008; Harter et al., 2002; Shuck and Wollard, 2010).

Importance of Employee Engagement

Few measurable benefits of Employee Engagement

a. Attrition rates in general or perhaps of a specific group of employees such as top talent
b. Sickness and absence levels
c. Performance as measured via your performance management system
d. Productivity or customer satisfaction levels
e. employees feeling valued
f. employees reporting clarity around their role and how they contribute to organisational success

Many Organisations through internal surveys have observed that Employee engagement plays vital role on major factors responsible for **"Organisational performance"** such as:

a. Turn over
b. Productivity
c. Profitability
d. Quality(Defects)
e. Customer Ratings
f. Safety Incidents
g. Shrinkages(thefts)
h. Absenteeism

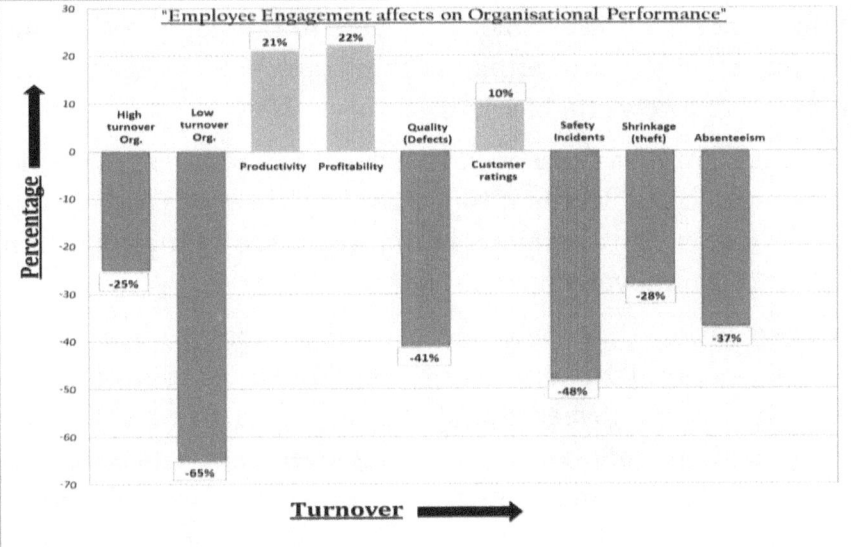

Figure 2: Employee engagement effects on organisational performance

Factors mentioned above pose challenge to Management in terms of various permutations of sole/coupled/combined effects on the Organisational performance.

Despite continuous and rigorous efforts percentage of engaged employees globally is very disappointing i.e 13% while different countries have different % of total employees as engaged employees depending upon the HR policies and how effective and relevant these HR policies are. Unites States of America has highest 30% engaged employees.

Researchers also have observed that Engagement of employee is not only outcome of HR Policies or Management Policies but it also depends on how much the employees are aware of their rights/entitlements rightfully. This factor makes huge impact on Country wise engagement trends. Hence USA has highest% of engaged employees as employees in USA are well aware and concerned about their rights and even the Labour courts/ tribunals too favour employee in disputes arising between employer and employees about their rights/entitlements.

Barriers to Employee Engagement

Before we go on to the enabler or drivers to Employee engagement and further on ways to enhance the Employee engagement it is important to know the barriers.

Various surveys done by industries through internal methods and external consultants it has come to light that Organisations working in air tight compartments are more vulnerable to low quotient of Employee engagement.

Organisation those with least internal communication with the employees and those neither have platform for communication link with the employees and take long time to realise, accept and implement policies to meet employee needs at large have very low Employee engagement points in any form of employee surveys.

During the research scholars have identified four broad categories of managers as "key moderators" whom business leaders consider vital to actual employee engagement; the moderators are observed across private & public sectors;

Few Leaders are not even familiar with the term "employee engagement". Many don't fully understand this concept and its possible benefits for the organisation.

Those, have interest in employee engagement, were not aware to handle this situation.

Just by agreeing to organisational needs for employee engagement, there is no surety that leaders will be able to implement the engagement strategies resulting into inability of organisational culture in creating engagement.

Groups of Leaders who support implement employee engagement, but suffer huge variability in opinion and commitment to implement employee engagement. Often importance of employee engagement is under reckoned. Few believe engagement is essential annual staff survey whose results need management's attention; Rest may feel a survey is merely a tool to identify employee engagement as key objective of organisational goal.

Based on various employee/organisational surveys following are listed as key barriers to Employee engagement:

1. Lack of employee –employer direct communication link as pointer to lack of transparency;
2. Paucity of funds/other means;
3. Suspicious/negative attitudes
4. Employees don't believe the messages they hear.
5. Top Management and lead manager blame team members for failures, bottle-necks, and ineffectiveness instead accepting own fault;
6. Lack of Right training;
7. Takes Longer to realise, accept and change behaviour, resulting in employees to lose heart.

4.5 ENGAGEMENT LEVELS

4.5.1 The Engaged, Disengaged and Actively Disengaged

It is very important for any organization to know the percentage of engaged, disengaged and actively disengaged employees of any organization. As per Gallup Poll report, Standard distribution of manpower of an organisation which strives for engaged employees through various initiatives normally constituted of $1/3^{rd}$ actively engaged 49–50% disengaged & 18% actively disengaged.

A study by consulting organisation Towers-Watson on engaged and disengaged employees showed a pattern of man power in the proportion 15% actively engaged, 65–70% moderately engaged, and only 15% disengaged employees. Upon revival of crashed economy capable and ambitious employees would come out of shell to explore new job opportunities, in such situation all the organisations would face high attrition unless organisation takes initiatives for aggressive employee engagement.

4.5.2. Actively Engaged Employees

Engaged employees in workplace parlance, are those take pride in their job profile & where they are working and completes all tasks in expected time frame. Such employees add value to the work ethics and work place environment of the organisation.

Engaged employees see challenge in a task which may bring benefits to the organisation, while others see the same as problem/laborious task.

Characteristics of Engaged Employees

Often it has been observed that Engaged Employees essentially exhibit following four factors

1. Enthusiasm – They are enthusiastic about work
2. Inspired – They are motivated by their leaders
3. Empowered – They are allowed to work the way they wish to
4. Confident – They are sure they can achieve excellence
5. They bring their friends into the Organisation
6. Beer outside the office starters
7. They stay updated about matters/policies etc concerning Organisation's business
8. They easily accept and adjust to new processes/policies

As per a survey by Gallup reported that engaged employees are well aware for their and expectations from their job role, are proud to do what they are assigned and the organisation they work for and use their creative skills for innovative ideas with full energy and enthusiasm.

Engaged employees are those who align their goals and efforts to achieve organisational goals and work diligently towards it. They are highly motivated and self-starter for any task assigned. They work on all the task with full passion, enthusiasm and creativity. They are the ones who are found in the top most list of succession planning for leading position of the organisation. The motivate and help co-workers too for better performance.

4.5.3. Disengaged Employees

Disengaged employees feel that their job is a deal between them and organisation for the time given by him for office and the salary they are being paid in return. They always feel that promoters give more time in office as they are owners and whole profit belong to them while we get only salary. Disengaged employees' donot volunteer for any new assignment and also re not willing to work extra. They are very particular about availing all the leave even if it delays the important task.

In many situations disengaged employees are those who were earlier engaged employees but during the race of career they fell out and suffered less increments and promotions resulting into loss of faith on supervisors and management.

Disengaged employees treat their job as commercial contract between them and employer wherein they are required to work for 8 hours in the office and that will make employer liable to pay salary to them. Most disengaged employees donot worry about performance about their team mates/sub ordinates and ae quite secretive about what they are doing so that no body learns to replace them. Some of the disengaged employees don't consider their jobs for long term with the employers and sometime even feels that they are either in a job/organisation they don't deserve in terms of their capability/dignity.

Hence, Dis-engaged employees, must be motivated to perform better as their conduct and attitude towards the organisation not only affect performance of the organisation but also team members/team. These trends sometime act as contagious disease which spread along the industry and spoils the organisational culture. At times dis-engaged employees infect even the loyalty of customers and potentially engaged employees.

Characteristics of Disengaged Employees

1. Perpetual Complainer
2. Makes Excuses
3. Lacks Enthusiasm
4. Doesn't Help Others & new joinees
5. Gossips around most of the times
6. Generally makes false claims/comments
7. Behaves as if they know it all
8. Not team members
9. Irresponsible
10. Takes no Initiative
11. Don't want to learn
12. No interest in self growth

4.5.4. Actively Disengaged Employees

Actively disengaged employees can become dangerous and contagious and harm for the performance of organization for their terrible role at work place which leaves none of the activity of employee performance vulnerable to its negative impact and pose serious threat to organisational culture too. They express & exhibit their dis contentment at work place in every word they speak, everyone they meet and many times even in social gathering using sarcastic language. They even go to the extent of mis leading customers & consumers and even praise for competitor's products.

They think and also voice their negative views on performance of almost everyone except employers for whom they use soft words stating that employers are being fooled/mis guided by opportunists etc and that they are worried about possible loses to the organisation. This soft language for employers by dis engaged employees are intentionally used, so that they don't face ire of the employers and their job is safe.

Kelly Services report shows that generally an organisation suffers by actively disengaged employees group which amounts to maximum upto 20% of the manpower, but negativity spread by them is much larger than their count in the work force and negatively affect output of team mates and organisational performance.

It is much more challenging but not impossible to re-engage actively disengaged employees.

Employee engagement affects the conviction of employees and organization's profits. Dan Crim and Gerard Seijts (2006) suggested ten C's of employee engagement which are as follows:

Clarity: Management need to communicate clearly as to vision of the organisation, goals set for their leaders and absolute clarity of their own goals so as to put in their best efforts to achieve the goals.

Career: All the ambitious employees expect meaningful and challenging job role and growth opportunities. To ensure that employees achieve their targets management ensure that employees have desired skills else it will be detrimental to motivation and employee engagement.

Congratulate: Generally employee's perceive that management is prompt in conveying failures/weakness but very late in conveying their success and even appreciating. They expect that the management must be as prompt in congratulating as in case of failure to induce and improve engagement.

Connect: Employee engagement points to connection among employees, bosses & senior management. Therefore, Management must respect their employees.

Communicate: Employees expect that the management & leaders define their expectations clearly. The leaders who wish that their team mates achieve the goals also provide processes and procedures to facilitate goal achievement of the organization by helping or guiding the employees as to how to achieve their personal goal, thus the organization goal.

Collaborate: Employees and teams who work with good rapport among themselves perform better than those individual & teams lack this very important aspect.

Contribute: Employee engagement can be improved by timely conveying feedback to the employees about importance of their role & performance for the organisational success. It also contributes to boost their self-esteem.

Control: Employees must be allowed to perform at judicious speed and autonomy as long as it is meeting the organisational goals. The freedom given to employees for decision making for their work helps not only to boost their confidence but also to increase employee engagement.

Confidence: Leaders with high performance scores and high ethical value generate high level of confidence among the employees and organisation which create employee engagement and gives competitive advantage to the organisation.

Credibility: Employees expect that their leaders expect and follow high ethical and moral values and desire similar actions from their team mates as they wish to take pride in referring to their social set up that they are working for such organisation.

4.6. DRIVERS TO EMPLOYEE ENGAGEMENT

Employee engagement is indispensable for an organization to improve the organization performance. To study drivers to employee engagement are the elements which are designed &initiated by HR department of an organization, that helps increase employee engagement levels also employee satisfaction.

Employee engagement is key factor to increase employee satisfaction and also utilizing full potential of employees.

In general, various internal and external surveys and seminar on Employee Satisfaction and Employee engagement, Employees/Respondents/Delegates suggested few key drivers to employee engagement inculcated and trickled down from to bottom in an organisation, areas under:

❖ Trust,

❖ Confidence and

❖ Belief;

❖ Communication; and

❖ Values

4.6.1. Engagement factors

4.6.1.1. Employee Satisfaction

Employee satisfaction is the indicator used to understand whether employees are happy, contented and their desires & needs at work are fulfilled. Many survey reports suggest that employee satisfaction plays key role in employee motivation, employee's achievements, and employee morale at workplace.

Employee satisfaction, unless measured alongside performance of employee it will generally show positive in most organization, while it may not be healthy count for an organisation if mediocre employees stay satisfied with your organisation's work environment.

One of the major indicators of Employee satisfaction in an organisation is "Attrition Rate". An organisation with high level of employee satisfaction will have reasonable Attrition rate which is considered healthy for organisational growth while an organisation facing with high Attrition rate, frequent employee unrests, strikes can always be identified by its low employee satisfaction index as in such organisation employees will not be motivated, committed and loyal to the organisation which directly relates to its poor employee engagement quotient.

Therefore, Employee engagement has direct relationship to Employee Satisfaction, it can also be termed as Employee Satisfaction is perfect complement to the Employee engagement.

Employee satisfaction factors fall under the following 6 basic categories:

- ❖ Work
- ❖ Employees
- ❖ Opportunities
- ❖ Compensation
- ❖ Policies & practices
- ❖ Quality of Life

The following model describes well the drivers of employee satisfaction

Figure 3: Employee Satisfaction Drivers

4.6.1.2 Employee engagement

Employee engagement cannot be achieved with out having satisfied employees hence employee satisfaction complement employee engagement, Drivers of employee satisfaction and employee engagement are also mostly same, engagement have few more factors as next level to satisfaction is morale and motivation once that is achieved engagement is achieved.

Employee Engagement drivers ruled by the following 6 basic factors:

❖ Work
❖ Employees
❖ Opportunities
❖ Total Rewards
❖ Organisation Practices
❖ Quality of Life

The following model describes well the drivers of employee engagement

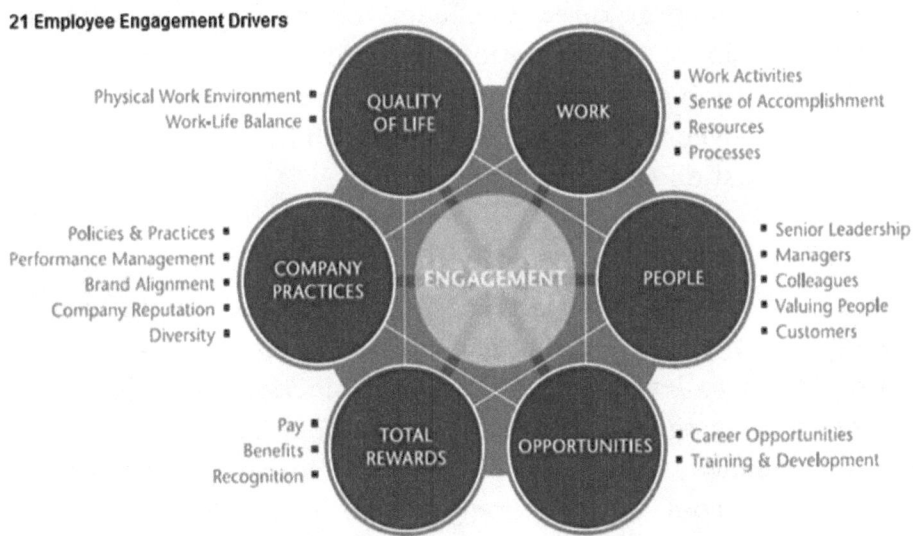

Figure 4: Employee Engagement Drivers

Work

The work related factors are significant contributors to employee engagement.

Work activities

Work activities include all the factors related to Job role and responsibilities.

The job role, job description which is given during the recruitment should match the job role and with the employee qualification and the skills and abilities. It was concluded in many surveys that right job given to the right person not only increases the output from the employees but also engages the employee to use his full potential to do his responsibilities at work place.

These activities have positive affect on the job satisfaction & increases employee performance. As employee is well aware of the job role which fits best with their skills and abilities and so it increases his engagement to the work.

Job Satisfaction directly effects job performance thereby effecting employee's organisational commitment. This means that the degree of job satisfaction has an impact on his performance and an employee who is fully satisfied with his job role will be in the lot of most engaged employees

Employees

The employees with whom the employee is working i.e. senior management, peers, colleagues, subordinates have significant contribution to levels of employee satisfaction. For e.g. If the senior management is easily approachable, employee can share their ideas and problems they face during completion of their project/goal and get timely advice to improve their work. Similarly if the co employees are of same mind-set it will be easier for them to work together on given project with the mutual understanding.

The communication link between all cadre of employees play vital role in employee engagement as this enhances transparency and clarity on the expectations through communication about the organization goal and management vision & mission. Therefore an organisation having internal communication as its strength achieves employee satisfaction much easier and quicker.

Total Rewards

Rewards and recognition plays significant role in building and enhancing employee morale and motivation to an extent that he/she start feeling engaged to the organisation and don't mind working extra if organisation so needed.

According to Kenneth Thomas there are two types of rewards, extrinsic rewards and intrinsic rewards.

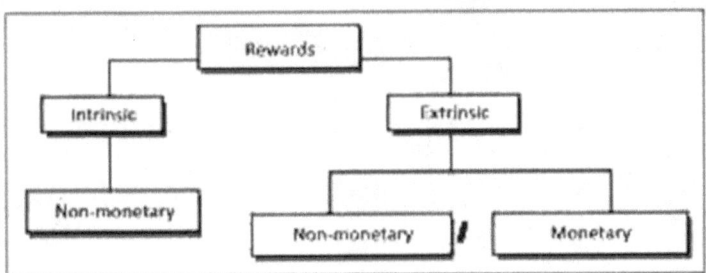

Figure 5: Rewards

Extrinsic rewards

Extrinsic rewards are usually financial rewards such as pay raises, bonuses, and benefits which are offered to employees for their performance. Benefits include non -financials in terms of developmental opportunity for career progress/performance improvement.

These are termed 'Extrinsic' being not part of employee's structure of job role and controlled/approved where needed, by someone other than employee himself. While "Intrinsic" rewards form part of job role construction/work place environment such as feeling of psychological wellness through performing well a meaningful work in terms of job satisfaction & motivation.

Extrinsic rewards were dominant when the job role was within the frame work of set norms & guidelines for achieving set goals and rewards were mostly monetary. Such job roles gave too little "Intrinsic rewards" and that too to very few categories of employees. Hence, during evolution times of industry "Extrinsic rewards" played role of main motivator, it was believed that only Pay a motivational factor for taking up/rejecting a job offer by an individual.

The diagram below shows impacts of Extrinsic types of rewards enumerated above

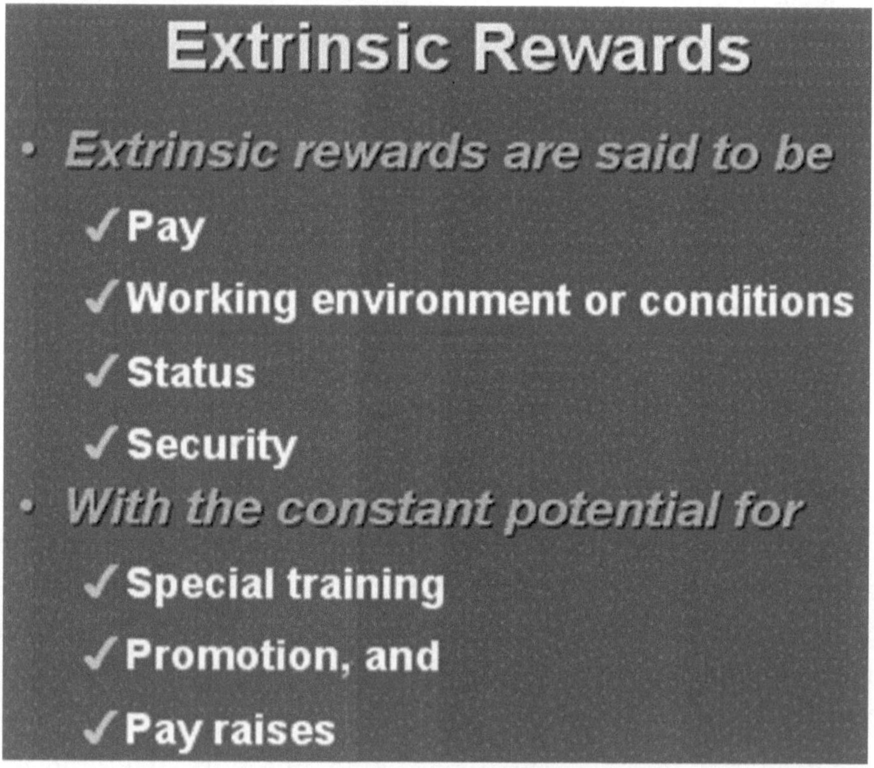

Extrinsic Rewards

- *Extrinsic rewards are said to be*
  - ✓ Pay
  - ✓ Working environment or conditions
  - ✓ Status
  - ✓ Security
- *With the constant potential for*
  - ✓ Special training
  - ✓ Promotion, and
  - ✓ Pay raises

Figure 6: Extrinsic Rewards

Intrinsic rewards

Intrinsic rewards are the self-esteem, recognition for the work done and the self-management and use of one's own skills & expertise to achieve the organisational goal. The self-management process requires employees make independent decision as to what is meaningful work that would be able to use their competence for achieving organisational goals and also give them feel good psychologically.

Intrinsic rewards keep employees self-motivated, independent in decision making and self-starter for any task improving their engagement levels.

The intrinsic rewards are

Sense of meaningfulness: These rewards are the feeling employees get from the job they perform to achieve meaningful and important organisational goal which makes them feel their role meaningful. Having done such tasks Employees feel that they were given opportunity to do something which is of vital importance for the organisation. Such opportunities make employees feel that they have received returns for their efforts and dedication to the meaningful task.

Sense of choice: These rewards are obtained when Employee is allowed to take independent decision as to choose, prioritise the task and also the approach to undertake these tasks. When such autonomy is given to the employee they develop feeling of ownership to the assignment and also take responsibility for success of its accomplishment or failure if it is not completed gainfully.

Sense of competence: This reward is obtained when the Employees professionally & psychologically feel that they are playing their roles very efficiently, diligently which meet the level of excellence set in the organisation. Such situation give them feeling of job satisfaction, personal & professional pride.

Sense of progress: This reward is achieved when Employees performance gains significance in organisational mission of achieving goals. Such rewards make them feel that their efforts are earning them respect and consequently they also foresee career growth in future. This also enhances their self-confidence in choosing, attempting and concluding the future tasks.

The diagram below shows impacts of intrinsic types of rewards enumerated above

The Four Intrinsic Rewards

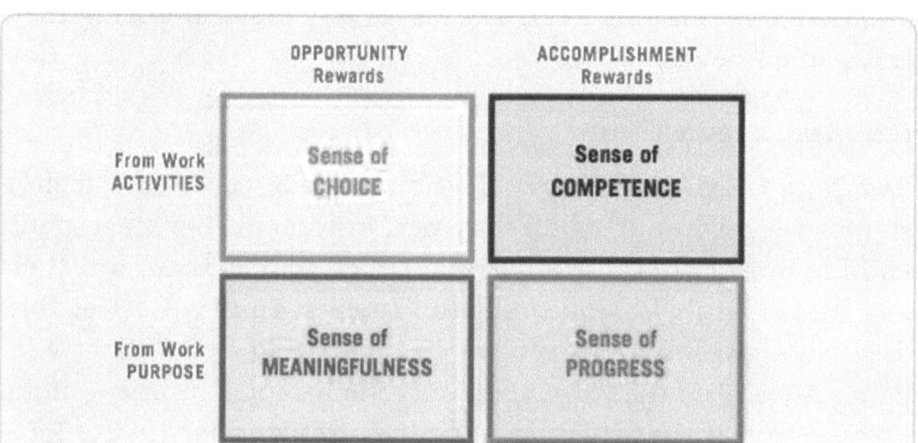

Figure 7: Intrinsic rewards

Combined impact of Extrinsic rewards and Intrinsic rewards

Employees who are in the category of engaged employees donot always expect monitory rewards from the organisation but settle for a good package of monitory, non-monitory and futuristic rewards in terms of benefits that ensures career progress/ performance improvement.

The diagram below shows some common impacts of both types of rewards enumerated above

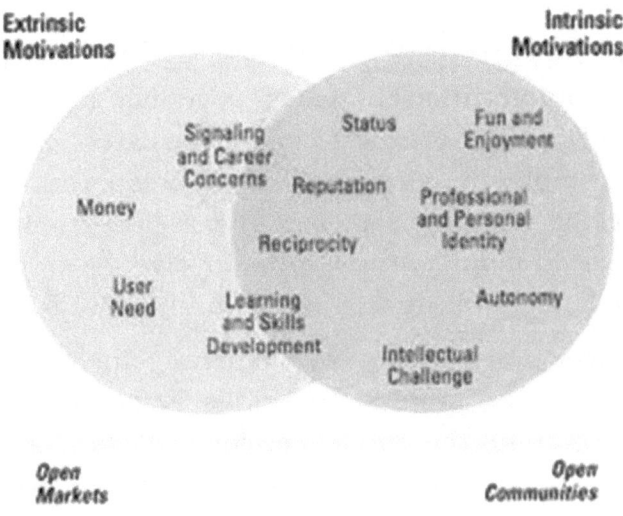

Figure 8: Motivation

Organisation practices

The different reward policies and practices are implemented in the organization. The reward policies act as a motivation to the employees. Various extrinsic reward policies/benefits are active benefits which include tangible benefits like performance pay and variable pay (e.g. overtime wages, commission to sales executives, different incentives), discounts etc. Other monetary benefits are retirement benefits, pension schemes, bonus, annual incentive, medical benefits for the employee and their family members, leave travel allowance, financial help for child education, for building own house and monetary help for other things.

Opportunity

Career development

Career Development is a universal process which includes self-learning & development making them competent in executing tasks to achieve desired goals and enhance their knowledge base & competency levels for desired career plan.

When an organization provides coaching and mentoring and skills development to ensure employee career growth in an effort to align employees' strengths and interests with that of the organization, the process is known as career development. The effective career development programs involve the employee, the manager and the organization in a comprehensive way.

Career development programs generally include technical training, basic skills, professional skills, supervisory skills. It is important to guide the employees for skill development and provide them the new doors for the progress in the organization by promoting them to higher position. It will not only help in retaining the employees but also increase the satisfaction level of them and so the engagement.

Training and development

Employees need to undergo training sessions facilitated by the organization to sharpen old skills & acquire new skill sets in the respective field.

Training and career development are very important in any Organisation that aims at progressing to achieve their goal. Training is the process of acquiring the essential skills required for a particular job. It targets specific goals, for example understanding a process and operating a certain machine or system. Career development, on the other side, gives emphasis on skills, which are applicable in a wide range of situations. This includes decision making, innovative thinking and managing employees.

Well-designed Training and Development activity in an Organisation benefits both Organisation and Employees simultaneously. At one side it help organisation develop its employees for better performance and higher retention, on other end it help employees enhance their skills which helps them improve performance and career growth.

A diagram below shows how Training and Development activity helps both Organisation and Employee collectively and individually.

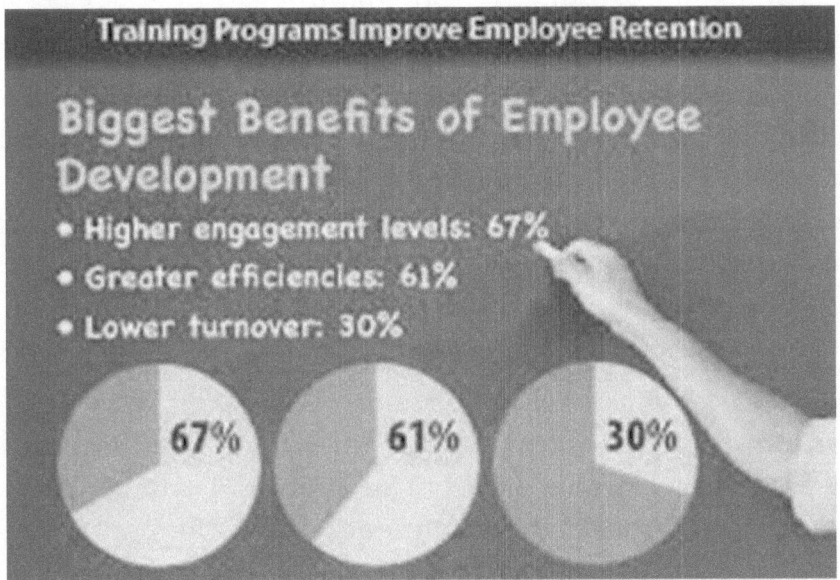

Figure 9: Training programs improve employee retention

Training helps in addressing employee weakness

Most employees have some weaknesses in their competency & capability, which obstruct them from giving the best individual out-put. Training helps in eliminating the weaknesses, by strengthening employees' skills. Well organized training and development program help employees not only to refresh skills and knowledge but also to bring them all to uniformly higher knowledge & skill level. This results in competency level of not only peon or few employees than that of whole workforce thereby making them more reliable. Hence the organization does not have to rely only on specific employees.

Improvement in employee's performance

A well trained employee becomes more educated about procedures for various tasks. The confidence is also boosted by training and development. The confidence comes from the fact that the employee is fully aware of his/her roles and responsibilities. It helps the employee to carry out the duties in better way and even find new ideas to incorporate in the daily execution of duty.

Consistency in duty performance: A well-organized training and development program gives the employees constant knowledge and experience. Consistency is of prime importance when it comes to organizations or Organisation's procedures and policies. This mostly includes ethics and administrative procedures during execution of duty.

In most organisations there are employees who would do specific tasks efficiently some times due to their interest in it, have incomplete knowledge about other tasks or to impress the bosses to come in lime light but in Human Resource parlance it cannot be termed as "Performance" as Performance means execution of tasks within allocated timeline, quality and objective with consistency.

Training and Development activity fills the gaps of knowledge base giving complete knowledge on a subject matter than selective thereby removing any anxiety of unknown task coming in hand resulting in enhancement of employee confident and performance.

Ensuring employee satisfaction: Training and development makes the employee confident about his job role as the Training resolves employee's anxieties of new tasks through improving knowledge and on the job trainings. Post training employee's performance improves and prepares them for new challenges, which makes him feel satisfied with the role they play in the organization. This is driven by the improved ability they gain to perform their duties. They feel they belong to the organization that they work for and the only way to reward it is giving the best services/performance they can offer.

Increased productivity

Through training and development, the employee acquires all the skills and knowledge needed in their day to day tasks. Employees can perform their duty more efficiently, thus improving overall productivity of the Organisation. They also gain new confidence for dealing and overcoming new challenges whenever they face them.

Improved quality of services and products

Training educate the Employees gain knowledge on standard process/methods to complete their tasks. They are able to maintain uniformity in the output they give. This results in an Organisation that gives satisfying goods or services in terms of quality of services and products achieving customer delight, akey business goal of organisations.

Reduced cost

Training and development results with optimal utilization of resources in the Organisation. This reduces wastage of resources i.e raw material, man power, utility etc thus save extra cost incurred by wastage of resources and reprocessing activities. As Training improves efficiency which also results into reduction in Accidents & defects. All the resources and machines are used economically & optimally which helps in reducing overall costs.

Reduction in supervision

Employees become more confident after gaining the necessary skills and knowledge. They become self reliant and require only little guidance as they perform their tasks. The supervisor not only can depend on the employee's decision to give quality output, but also his burden of constantly having to give directives on what should/shouldnt be done, will be relived.

A diagram below shows how Training benefits employee as an individual, as team members professionally and commercially.

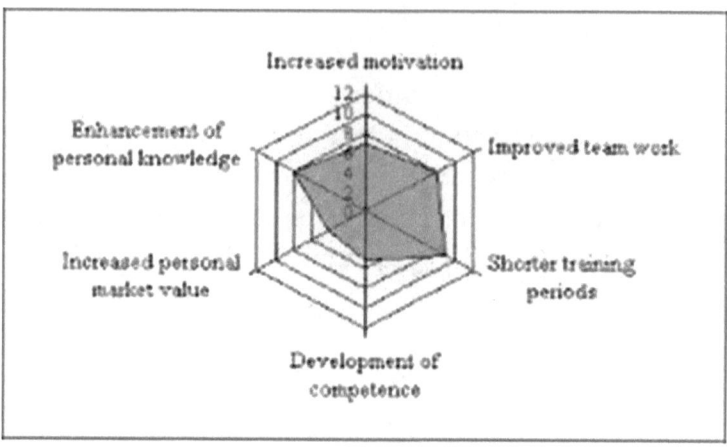

Figure 10: Training benefits

Quality of life

Work/life balance

Work-life balance is important aspect for an organisation to have employee's continued to be engaged with their job role and resultantly with the organisation as this will not cause burnout/ physical-emotional fatigue in employees. The employees who are able to manage work – life balance by dividing their time and energy between work and personal life and giving appropriate time to both the aspects able to attain desired job satisfaction and employee engagement. Employees unable to handle this challenge are vulnerable to demotivation and burnout.

An appropriate work-life balance level is individual's approach & depends upon rationalisation of personal - professional objectives. Few employees donot find them-selves comfortable working for extended hours daily. Whereas, others don't feel so working long days. Work life balance is always in variable state and changes as per the situation, many a times daily changing situation. Work-life balance is balancing the factors that influence them i.e tasks, control, technology, manager behaviour, flexible working policies as well as drivers of employee engagement.

Work place environment & managerial behavioural factors affect work-life balance and leave most significant impressions on employees mind sets. Successful managers are those craft their own work-life balance. After the success they become role model for themselves, guide juniors, support those need to excel. Such employees and leaders initiative create active work-life balance environment which help and support everyone.

Most organisations who value work life balance ensure that employees are well equipped to undertake their tasks independently so that they can finish tasks with in expected time frame and are also able to maintain work life balance. Organisations also conduct training on time management, stress management etc to help achieve work life balance more efficiently.

Organisations also adopt activities such as flexi timing, work from home, provide better IT infrastructure, video conferencing to reduce travel, health & fitness facilities/subsidies etc which allows employee to maintain work life balance.

Few researchers have found following work-life balance model working well with employees of all levels across globe with minor specific job/industry scenario customisation such as employees on senior executive level need more time at Office/Work than for children as their children are grown up and also time for sleep as with age sleep reduces etc.

The table and pie chart below shows what has been most commonly distribution of 24 hrs by those who feel they are able to maintain work life balance as per the data collected by few surveys carried out by health consultants:

Work-Life Balance

Activities	Hours at each Activity (approx)	Percentage of 24 Hours at each Activity (approx)
Sleep	7	29
Office	9	38
Travel to and from Office	3	13
Time with Kid/Pet	1	4
TV/Movies	1	4
Dinner/Break fast	2	8
Misc	1	4
Total	24	100

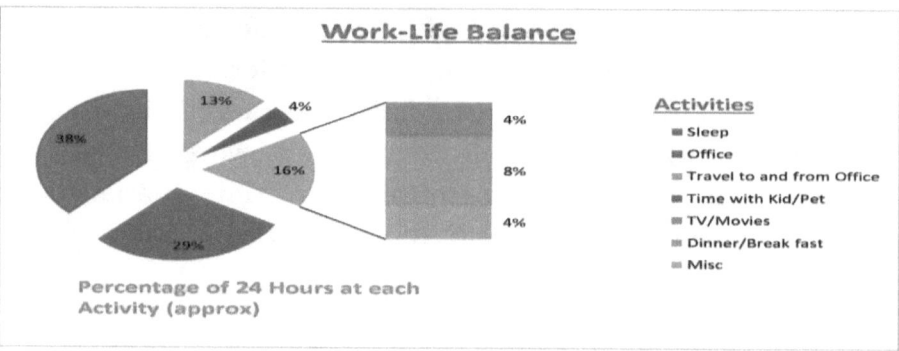

Figure 11: Work life balance

Researchers in their reports quoted that though work life balance is important aspect for employee engagement but in many cases, employees have ignored this for better career opportunity and recognition for good performance broadly for 03 key reasons as below:

1. 'Good' work-life balance is highly subjective & depends upon individual's preferences. Many employees are averse to extended hours of working, while rest don't have similar opinion and consider part of their duty and dedication if at all they need to spend extra hours at work.

2. 'Right' work life balance is a variable factor, at times individual's preferences differ for every situation/day.

3. Work-life balance is outcome and usually impacted by factors which influence employee engagement such as

autonomy, meaningful assignments, technical know-how, supervisor's conduct, flexi timing, – while this itself is driver of employee engagement.

Physical work environment

Physical work environment has significant influence on employee's performance, attitude towards organisation, Loyalty and job satisfaction, engagement levels and well-being feeling.

The key factors that have direct impact on above are location, layout, design of the building with specific features e.g. ventilation, room temperature, noise levels, furniture, office equipment etc.

Various study report on work place environment concluded that the work place environment has huge impact on the performance of employees as it gives them apt physical comfort, stress free vision, comfortable breathing space & comfortable room temperature which improve their out put, as, such environment keep them health and motivated.

Many organisation conduct internal and external surveys about the work place environments in general across the industry and some even specific benchmarks for a particular business segment i.e. IT sector, Media etc and these inputs are used to ensure that the employees are given desired work place environment.

As Customer centric strategy plays vital role in market dominance for an organisation, Employee centric approach/policies not only improve productivity and profitability but also gives the organisation unique identity as "Best Place to work or Best Employer" etc. This management approach helps them retain the talent and also attract new talents thereby achieving longer & competitive employee life cycle in the organisation. Following Environmental hazards require consideration in any workplace:

Ambiance: A cramped sitting place, old fashioned office equipments, faded & tasteless wall colours, unpolished and obsolete design furniture are few factors contribute towards office ambience to a great extent and become a big reason for employees demotivation and low work place esteem, directly effects employee engagement.

Work place Ambiance plays important role in enhancing employee morale, employee delight & pride which contributes towards employee engagement.

The management approach behind is very pragmatic as in current business scenario employees spend more time in office than at home, hence they should feel as happy, contended as if they are "at home"

The Ambience encourages employees to refer their organisation as one of the best place to work and recommend good talents to their organisation.

There are certain organisations such as Media, IT, Fashion, Garment particularly which invest huge money in designing & decorating their offices, studios, meeting rooms, canteen, work places matching with their international counter-parts/ competitors, as they firmly believe if that is not done they will not be appropriately manage the talents in terms of retention, performance, morale, motivation & delight and will not be able to attract new talent.

Noise: Noise is considered an intruder into peaceful environment, it not only create undue stress on ears but also make environment cluttered with unwanted noise which many times absorb even emergency message resulting into catastrophic.

Noise at work place can cause mis-communication, lack of communication which may lead to important instructions/alerts not reaching the receiver which may affect performance/safety.

Lighting: Proper light is a big factor in any event/situation whether it is work place/social place/religious place etc as it allows the people to see things rightly help them draw right inference at right time. Dim lighting puts extra stress on eyes and at times become intolerable for an individual to perform duties. Proper light not only helps reader read the full content but also help them comprehend it correctly.

Ventilation, thermal comfort and air quality: Ventilation is very important factor which deals with the dust, fume, odour, temperature control & balance and compose the environment of any place and also of work place environment. On negative side, dust can cause asthma, breathing problems and even allergies in eyes & skins. Fumes and gases too can cause skin and lungs infections while heat can make one uncomfortable at work and cause de hydration, suffocation & fatigue.

Vibration: Vibrations to any part of body or whole body vibration can cause severe limb impairment partially/fully due to disturbance in the blood flow in vessels. At times vibration at job role causes premature fatigue/physical disability due to stress on a particular part of body specially one loaded with muscular/bonny part. Vibrations in abdomen area can cause stomach pain, gastrointestinal ailments and even problems in spinal cord. Vibration in hand tools can cause numbness and many other types of ailments.

Radiation: Sun rays emit ultra violet rays which are very harmful for eyes and skin. Doctors suggest that exposure to ultra violet rays can cause skin cancer and also cataract in eyes. Hence protection from excessive exposure to Sun is must. Exposure to Sun also can cause de hydration and fatigue.

4.6.1.3. Job satisfaction

Job satisfaction is emotional state of employees as to how content they are in their job role and how much they like their job. It is evaluated on two dimensions, their overall satisfaction level in the job and also satisfaction level at different aspect of job role.

Author Spector listed down 14 common aspects for job satisfaction: Appreciation, Communication, Co-employees,

Fringe benefits, Job conditions, Nature of the work, Organization, Personal growth, Policies and procedures, Promotion opportunities, Recognition, Security, and Supervision.

Affective job satisfaction level is the degree of satisfaction they get from the job while Cognitive job satisfaction is the satisfaction employees receive from various aspects of the job. Cognitive job satisfaction can be uni-dimensional and also multi-dimensional depending upon whether it deals with one or more aspects of job role.

Job satisfaction affect multi-dimension aspects of individual's experience at workplace and work –life balance opportunities. Job satisfaction is linked with employee well-being, work pressure, autonomy at job role, work life balance etc.

(Locke, 1976) quoted Job satisfaction as level of happiness employee gets from various aspects of job and also the attitude employee has towards the job.

There are three components to job satisfaction: evaluative, cognitive and behavioural. The evaluative parts deal with liking or disliking the job, for example: "I love my job and what I do" or "I do not like my job & I am not happy in my position". Cognitive aspect is related with the different beliefs about the job, e.g. "My job is very stressful, but the salary is very good" or "My job is not much challenging, but it is comfortable". Lastly, the behavioural aspect looks at how each person is susceptible to act, e.g. motivation, punctuality, hardworking, and organization. If these three components are combined, it will help to the job and can affect employees' overall attitude and behaviour.

Some employees look forward to going to work and really take pleasure and pride in what they do. There are some employees who cannot stand their job and are completely dissatisfied with their job. There are three general categories that cause an employee to be satisfied and dissatisfied with their job. These are-job characteristics, social comparison and disposition.

Job characteristics comprises of things like skill and task identity and working conditions such as stress, workload and the relationships that employee have with their co-employees. Social comparison comprises of designation, authority etc while disposition comprises of esteem and pride given by the job role.

The most popular measure of job satisfaction assesses how employees feel about the job along five dimensions: type of work, pay, promotional opportunities, supervision and co-employees (Smith, Kendall & Hulin, 1969). Social comparison mainly deals with relationship with co-employees. Attitudes are contagious and affect everyone at the workplace. Employees will be more satisfied if their co-employees are satisfied, and unfortunately, it goes the same for the opposite as well (PSU WC, 2013). Disposition refers to the fact that some individuals are prone to be more satisfied or dissatisfied, despite the nature of the job or the social environment (PSU WC, 2013).

Factors contributing towards Employee Job satisfaction

Many consulting organisations and operational organisations have been carrying out surveys to understand the factors which contribute towards achieving Employee satisfaction. Various surveys have brought out different factors but following factors have been found common among almost all the surveys:

a. Meaningful work
b. Pay
c. Benefits
d. Job security
e. Opportunities to growth
f. Safety at work place
g. Relationship with co-employees
h. Relationship with management
i. Fun at workplace

Dispersion of above factors is depicted below in pie chart for better understanding

Employee's Job Satisfaction Balancing Wheel

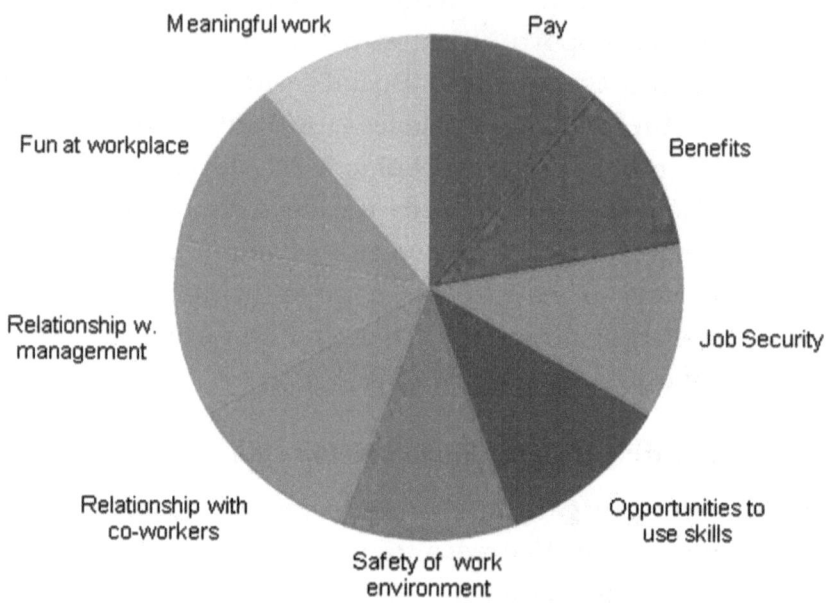

Figure 12: Employee's Job satisfaction balancing wheel

The Importance of Job Satisfaction

Job satisfaction is related to various factors e.g performance, absenteeism, & attrition. Job satisfaction influences individual's approach & conduct. Approach & conduct of individuals can motivate/de motivate them to be dedicated or not dedicated at all towards his role. Job satisfaction impacts individual's well-being too. Hence, dis-satisfaction at job role may result into dis-satisfaction in other parts of life too.

As per author Luthan (1998) various aspects of job satisfaction are:

a. Job satisfaction is employee's emotional response to experience at work place which can be interpreted by his actions & approach to the organisation and job role.

b. Job satisfaction levels vary as per the employee's satisfaction level through rewards in return to their efforts to achieve goals. Often employees compare their rewards with employee of other department without comparing the goals & achievements, which sometimes gives dis-satisfaction.

c. Job satisfaction is employee's reaction to various aspects of job in terms of compensation, benefits, work place environment, manager's conduct and rewards etc attached to the job.

4.6.1.4 Employee performance

The link between job satisfaction and job performance has controversial history 1924–1933 Hawthorne studies (Naidu, 1996) helped researchers to know connection between performance & satisfaction. Various researchers have disparagingly studied idea of "Happy employee is productive employee". Iaffaldano and Muchinsky (1985) surveyed and found a weak job satisfaction and job performance. While Organ (1988) in his research discovered that due to less information on job performance, the strong bond between performance &satisfaction could not be established. Organ (1988) observed that inclusion of Organisational citizenship in job performance's definition will improve connection between satisfaction and performance.

Judge, Thoreson, Bono, and Patton (2001) reported that correction in sample and measurement errors enhances connection between job satisfaction & job performance increased upto 30%. Relationship between job satisfaction and job performance varies depending upon complexity of job. (Saari & Judge, 2004).

Researcher Michelle Jones reviewed 03 case studies which included 74 different investigations of job satisfaction & job performance of Twelve thousand employees, in 2006. She further said that researchers have found positive but weak connection between job satisfaction & job performance.' Jones emphasised on need to find connection between satisfaction in life in all aspects and performance at work (Bright, 2008).

4.6.1.5 Employee absenteeism

(Cheloha & Farr, 1980) said that employee absenteeism and job satisfaction link is most desirable topic among researchers. (Johns, 1997) said that relationship between absenteeism and job satisfaction is virtually zero as an unsatisfied employee either will report sick or opt for job change. Researchers also suggested that unsatisfied employees will be averse to come to job even if they are well while satisfied employee will attend office even if they are not well, they hardly remain absent.

4.6.1.6 Employee Turnover

Carsten and Spector, 1987) reported 24% correlation between employee turnover and job satisfaction. Higher turn over of employees is triggered by economic slowdown also when organisations start sacking non/poor performing employees, while a satisfied employee may resign only in pressing situation. Hence relationship between employee turnover and job satisfaction is beyond a point which can be measured.

Application of Job Satisfaction in the Workplace

Importance of job satisfaction in an organisation is tough to comprehend due to its circumstantial and individualistic nature. The desires of employees from their jobs are different. For example, one employee think his/her salary is most important, while another may think autonomy most important. Unfortunately, only one aspect alone will not affect an employee's job satisfaction.

According to Syptak, Marsland, and Ulmer (1999), there are numerous aspects of a job that an organization can manage to increase satisfaction in the workplace, these are as follows,

Organisation Policies – Policies that are fair, clear and applied equally to all employees will decrease dissatisfaction. Therefore, clarity and fairness are important and help in long way in improving employee attitude. For example, if an organization has a policy for lunch breaks that are of the same length and time for everyone, employees will consider this as the norm and it will help cut down on wasted time and so the low productivity.

Salary/Benefits – If employee salaries and benefits are comparable to other organization salaries and benefits or as per the industry standards, will help raise satisfaction. If an Organisation wishes to produce a competitive product they must also offer competitive wages. In addition, this also helps in reducing turnover, as employees will be more satisfied when paid competitive wages as opposed to being underpaid.

Interpersonal/Social Relations – Allowing employees to develop a social aspect to their job not only increases satisfaction but also develop a sense of teamwork. Co-employee relationships can also benefit the organization as a whole. Teamwork is a very important aspect of organization productivity and success. When employees are allowed to develop relationships at workplace they care more about pulling their own weight and not letting co-employees down.

Working Conditions – Providing all the required facilities and equipment and making sure those employees have adequate personal workspace, helps in decreasing dissatisfaction. An unsatisfied employee is a frustrated employee while faulty equipment helps increasing the frustration in trying to get work done.

Achievement – When the employees are given job role matching to their talents, it may enhance satisfaction. When employees are in appropriate role and feel a sense of challenge & achievement, their talents will be in line with the goals best suited for them and in line with the organization goal as well.

Recognition –Providing the time to employees to acknowledge a job well done can increase the chance of employee satisfaction. Constructive and positive feedback boosts an employee's morale and keeps them working in the right direction.

Autonomy – Giving employees the freedom of decision making and ownership of their work may help increase satisfaction. Job satisfaction can result when an individual knows they are responsible for the outcome of their work.

Advancement – The employees who show high performance and loyalty, if organization allows them room to advance will help ensure satisfaction. A new sense of responsibility may often increase job satisfaction in an employee.

Job Security – Security of Job plays major role in employee's level of satisfaction at job, especially in times of economic uncertainty. If an employee is given the assurance that their job is secure will help most likely increase job satisfaction.

Work-life Balance Practices – In times where the average household is changing it is becoming more important for an employer to recognize the delicate balancing act that its employees perform between their personal life and work life. Policies that are in tune with common personal and family needs play essential role to maintain job satisfaction.

Organizational Commitment – Organisational commitment is employee's approach towards organisation and is indication of their loyalty and dedication to the organisation.

Beckeri, Randal, and Riegel (1995) suggested 03 dimensions to measure organisation commitment:

1. Strong desire to continue working for an organization;
2. Level of Initiative to dedicate intensified hard work as representative of Organization;
3. Will to define and accept set organisation's values & goals.

Northcraft and Neale (1996), defined Organisational commitment as employee's loyalty to organization, and to continue it they feel free to convey concerns to the management for organisational success & well-being.

The authors further stated that Organizational commitment is result of contribution of number of factor, including organizational factors (job role & manager's leadership style); personal factors (age, length of service in organization, disposition, internal/external control attributions); non-organizational factors (availability of alternatives).

Mowday, Porter, and Steer (1982) refer organisational commitment as employee's belongingness & loyalty to organisation. They listed down 03 three constituents of Organisational commitment:

a. Employee's alignment level to organisation's goals &core values ;
b. Employee's willingness to remain associated with the organization;
c. Employee's keenness to exhibit endeavours as responsible representative of the organization.

4.6.1.7. Employee well-being

Employee wellbeing has been accepted by Industry as key factor for organisation's continued growth and enhanced performance. Employee's experience at work place motivates him to put in extra and dedicated hard work towards achieving organisational goals in return for organisation's initiative to care for their vital need of organisational work environment.

Employee wellbeing also triggers competitive spirit among employees to performance harder and better than before and than others which ultimately results in better organisational performance. Employees with high level of wellbeing are very dedicated and loyal and they don't take even leave unless they are really immovable as they are concerned to their role and its importance for organisational performance unlike employee's who don't have any feeling of belongingness to the organisation. Employees having high well-being scores are open to accept change and always think out of box for the organisational growth.

There are 03 types of employee well-being:

(1) Subjective wellbeing (2) workplace wellbeing and (3) psychological well-being.

Employee well-being is directly linked to employee performance and employee turnover it is considered as pointer to organizational well-being.

Definitions of Employee Well-being

As per Oxford English Dictionary (2nd ed., revised 2005) "Well-being - The state of being comfortable, healthy or happy."

Dr. Juniper explained employee wellbeing as component of employee's wellbeing as a whole while working for the Organisation & which can be improved by organisational interventions.

"Employee wellbeing is resultant of their happiness while at work."

"Employee wellbeing is outcome of their views, feelings & perceptions about their jobs & organization."

4.6.2 Drivers of employee well-being

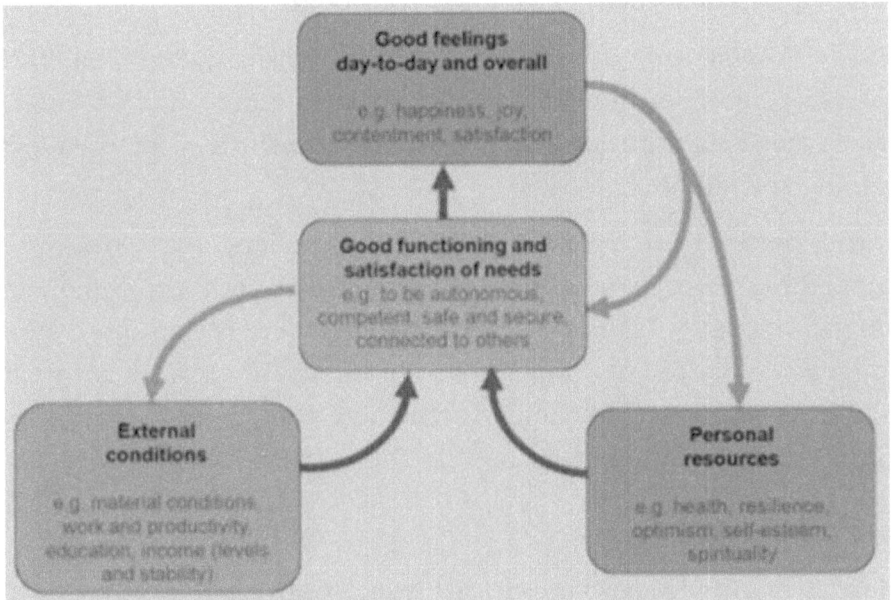

Figure 13: Drivers of employee well-being

It is not employee engagement alone but Well-being too which motivates employees to work for the organisation with commitment and loyalty towards achieving organisational goals

Employee Well-being is not spontaneous/natural reaction by employees for employee engagement activities by the organisation but every organisation need to study various factors which would drive employee to the develop feeling of well-being.

Most of the engagement activities conducted by organisations are with an objective to have impacts on Drivers to well-being thereby in order to achieve organisation goals.

Based on various studies and researches following have been found to be Drivers of well-being:

Personal resources – It is the experience of employee for organisational initiatives for his health & hygiene, morale & confidence, work rule flexibility & work-life balance. Hence the organisations who take care of these concerns of employees achieve higher levels of employee well being.

Good functioning at work: Regular performance feedback system, good conduct of manager, trust and cooperation among employees and autonomy at work place are the key factors affect employee wellbeing.

The experience of work: Employee's experience at work, play important role in developing well-being feeling among employees. As the Industry is working innovatively few researchers have suggested leaders to handle employee well-being as strategic goal and suggested to tackle it through plan, execute, monitor, map, improve and sustain as it is the responsibility of leaders.

4.6.2.1. Mental health

Mental health is very important constituent of employee well-being; it is a positive factor than interpretation of no signs of employee's bad attitude towards the organisation.

Mental health has been favourite corporate topic for study among researchers and clinical practitioners as they have done extensive work on this over a period of time.

Many authors quoted mental health as result of favourable organizational behaviour, which induces optimism & flexibility among the employees (Luthans 2002; Luthans and Youssef 2004, 2007), and researchers (Cameron ; Caza 2004; Cameron et al. 2003) also linked mental health with conducive work environment across organisation.

Researchers (Diener 1984; Keyes 2002; Ryff 1989) were the pioneers in studying wellbeing as psychological element and developed a comprehensive model. Researchers (Wright and Cropanzano 1997) stated that study on wellbeing has been very limited as it has always been linked only to employee's job satisfaction.

4.6.2.2. Subjective well-being

Researchers (Diener et al. 1999; Busseri et al. 2007) suggested that SWB is defined within the scope of individual's overall satisfaction level in life through organisational behaviour, its positive affect of high score & negative affect of low score.

Subjective well-being (SWB) refers to how employees experience and evaluate their lives and specific domains and activities in their lives. Over the past decade, interest in knowledge about SWB (also called "self-reported wellbeing") has increased markedly among researchers, national statistical offices, politicians, the media, and the public. The value of this information lies in its potential role in mapping social, economic, & health of people (Layard, 2006; Krueger et al., 2009).

Keyes' (2002, 2005, 2007) refers study of wellbeing as mental health is product of positive emotions and positive role play by employee. Happiness from job role is resultant of dedicated efforts which enhances happiness and reduces pains (Waterman 1993). SWB, is state of mind filled with positivity gained through real life experience. SWB is not an imitative form of happiness and positive emotions (Waterman 1993), self-actualisation (Maslow 1968)and self-determination (Ryan and Deci 2001). Ryff's (1989) said SWB is signification of psychological well-being (PWB) indicating good mental health.

4.6.2.3. Positive feeling

Generally Happiness and SWB have been used by researchers as two sides of the coin but SWB has always been known as broad definition of happiness/well-being. Researcher (Diener 2000) reported that happiness has three dimensional constituents i.e over all happiness in life giving mental happiness, positive influence and absence of negative affect constituents.

(Ryan and Deci 2001) stated that happiness has two dimensions i.e Hedonic happiness means one that is acquired through physical or bodily pleasures/comforts and reducing discomforts in material life/life style, while Eudemonic happiness means fulfilment through individual's own efforts using talent and also spiritual fulfilment which is somewhere closer to Maslow (1968) theory of self-actualisation and Roger's (1961) theory of fully accomplished individual. Author Waterman (1993) stated that individual's happiness is at peak when his life is full of feeling of fulfilment through fair means.

Ryff & Keyes (1995) referred happiness comes from sovereignty, personal growth, self-confidence, meaningful life, climatic positivity and good personal relations, while Ryan and Deci's (2000) advocated happiness & psychological growth linked to sovereignty, proficiency & affiliation. (Ryan and Deci 2000) with initial empirical research supporting this view (e.g. Peterson et al. 2005) suggested that eudemonic happiness is resultant of growth of individual's strength and virtues.

4.6.2.4. Psychological Well-Being (PWB)

PWB is a feel good factor in individuals which deals with over all happiness i.e. happiness in career/work place and happiness in personal & social life. It is believed that for long lasting happiness, happiness need not exist all the time but should be mixed of happiness and pains, disappointments etc and one's ability to deal with change of situation else it is believed to be intervening with individual's competency at work place.

Health is an overall well-being which includes physical, mental and social happiness and not just absence of any ailment/incapability (WHO, 1948). WHO also redefined positive mental health as mental state which allows individual to rely upon their capability, enable them handle stress and perform gainfully to the society (WHO, 2001).

The main reasons of new definition of mental health are as under:

1. Realisation for need of independent study of positive well-being is much beyond just absence of ill-being;

2. Differentiate between following dimensions which help enhance psychological
   Wellbeing:
   a. Treating disorder when it is present;
   b. Preventing disorder from occurring; and
   c. Enhancing well-being;

3. Well proven that drivers of well-being and ill-being are different.

4. Belief that with explosion of population, due to work stress, focus may be more on reducing common mental & behavioural issues than on treatment & prevention of disorder.

4.6.3 Organization performance

Organizational performance is the measurable results of efforts put in by work force of an organisation in achieving the targeted goals, in terms of productivity and profitability.

Richard et al. (2009) said organizational performance includes following:

1. Financial performance (profits, return on assets, return on investment, etc.);

2. Product market performance (sales, market share, etc.); and

3. Shareholder returns (total shareholder returns, Financial value addition, etc.).

Many researchers have reported that there is need for measuring performance in all the key functions i.e strategic planning, operations, finance, legal, & organizational development. In doing so many organizations have adopted BSC (Balanced Score Card) approach of performance monitoring & mapping where in four perspective goals are set and performance is measured against them i.e financial, internal business process, learning & growth, customer satisfaction.

4.6.4. Relationship between Employee engagement and organization performance

Researchers have claimed that employee engagement and organisational performance are logically connected, engaged employees behave as ambassador for the organisation as they quote their organisation as best place to work while disengaged employees quote organisation as average/poor/worst place of work. Various research data show 53% employees quote their organisation as top/best performing were highly engaged employees while 8% are those quote their organizations under-performing were engaged. Hence, Organisations must proactively communicate with employees about the organisational performance so that right message goes to all the employees enhancing employee engagement levels, to society & market, thus communication will reach to prospective employees too.

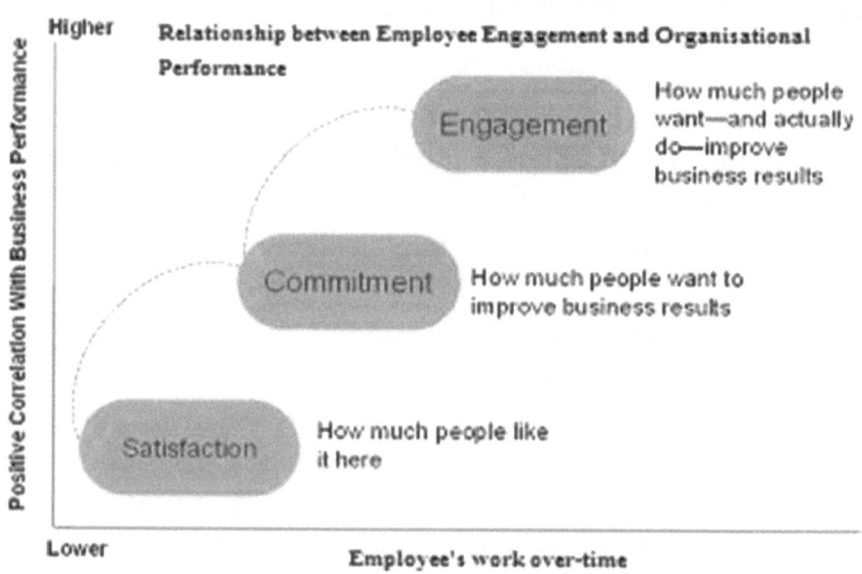

Figure 13(a): Employee's work over time

Figure 14: Relationship between employee engagement and organizational performance

4.6.5. Organization culture

Organisation culture is formed by combined effects of interaction levels between employees & management and also actions & functioning style of leadership.

Organisation culture takes shape by upbringing and employee attitude towards Organization and also employee's conduct while working, simultaneously leadership styles of management and Organisation's vision & mission, core values, policies, processes, communication styles, ethics, transparency etc.

The above cultural indictors are given to the new joinees at the time of joining during the induction process.

Organisation culture sets the discipline & behavioural guidelines for employees while mutual interaction, and also with customers, vendors & other stake holders.

Ravasi & Schultz (2006) quoted organizational culture as beliefs which influences communication, working styles and interactions with in and out side the organisation by employees and management teams. There are cases where in organisations have common cultural trends and also organisations with conflicting cultural trends for different teams due to generation/ technological gaps.

Schein (1992), Deal; Kennedy (2000); Kotter (1992) quoted that many organisations are surviving well despite having different internal cultures termed as sub cultures.

Author Needle (2004), stated that organizational culture indicates values, beliefs &ethics applicable to all the employees across the grades which emerges due to organisational growth journey, product category, age of technology, market scenario, &management strategy, cultural upbringing of employees within organisation, management functioning style.

4.6.5.1. Essentials of Organisation culture

Communication

Communication is an important ingredient of creating a strong corporate culture. When employees are given opportunity and platform to communicate freely, they instead just venting frustration give very constructive inputs/feedbacks/opinions.

In turn Management must respect such inputs and take some decisions and communicate to employees that their inputs are valued and taken cognisance of. That will develop transparency in the system. Such culture can also encourage participation, engagement and sharing innovative ideas.

Authority

In organisations with centralised working environment, employees feels helpless in most situation as he is not allowed to take decision and begin to feel detached from work life.

Hence, organisations having work environment of delegation of authority to employees as per their cadre allow them to take decisions while discharging duty and prevent the "Us vs. Them" mind-set. This work environment also improves employee morale and commitment to the organisation.

Safety

If employees don't feel safe at work, they will not to be engaged in work. Employees worried about job security, harassment by other employee, undermine everything they try to do etc.

To create a comfortable and safe work environment, organisations need to build culture that does not tolerate harassment in any form by giving employees procedures for reporting such incidents and take complaints seriously so that they feel protected and able to focus on their work.

Opportunities for Growth

An organisation can provide opportunities to employees to learn new skills, take new responsibilities through training & development and career planning/promotion policies keep set criteria to get such opportunities in a transparent manner.

Such organisations are successful in removing redundancies and job stagnation among the whole talent pool. With such policies and opportunities for learning & growth organisation can expect enhanced employee morale, motivation, thereby enhancing employee engagement.

Sustainable employee engagement

In current too competitive, pressured and fast-paced work environment & business scenario Organisations need to not only achieve Engagement, but also achieve "sustainable Employee engagement" to sustain organisational performance.

Sustainable engagement can also be defined as intensity of connectivity between employees and organisation. It is based on three core elements:

❖ Limits of employee's discretionary power/authority in decision making while doing duty to achieve job targets (being engaged).

❖ Work place culture which creates & enhances ways to performance (well being enabled)

❖ Employee's Experience at work place which may develop feeling of comfort promotes a well-being (feeling energized). Researcher have found that conducive work environment energizes employees by promoting their physical, emotional and social well-being.

Five Drivers to Sustainable Employee Engagement

Priority areas of focus	Behaviours and actions that matter to employees
Leadership	Effective leadership inducing growth
	Willingness to address employees well-being
	Alignment and efforts to align with the organisation's core values
	Gains employees trust & confidence
Stress, Balance and Work load	Controllable stress levels at work
	Healthy work life balance
	Right team size for targeted goals
	Elastic work provisions
Goals and Objectives	Employees comprehends:
	Organisation's strategic goals
	Steps they need to take to reach the goals
	Job role orientation to organisational goals

Supervisors	Proper work allocation as per skill sets
	Committed & reliable
	Mentor employees help them perform better
	Respectable dealing with employees
Organisation's Image	A big brand name in masses & public
	Mirror image of honesty &integrity

Relationship between Employee engagement and Organisational Culture

Organisation culture plays major role in enhancing employee engagement levels in an organisation.

The culture of organization can have a huge impact on its employees. A positive, open culture creates trust and loyalty spirit in employees, developing in them passion for their job and a commitment to the organisation.

In such organisations Employees feel comfortable working culture thereby help getting engaged in their jobs and organisations, which can inspire enthusiasm and productivity. Investing time and money to create a strong culture, make an organisation more competitive and profitable, as such organisations will be able to develop and retain big pool of engaged employees.

Ways to enhance Employee engagement

Though employee engagement is vast and critical issue to deal with as this directly effect organisation performance, hence set of its drivers may also be different and on the way forward, ways to its enhancement too will have different factors for different organisation.

However, based on reports by various researcher as to how to enhance employee engagement following ways are considered universally applicable:

1. Assign organisation values
2. Have teams create their own set of values
3. Encourage personal projects
4. Assign a buddy/mentor for every newcomer
5. Have themed office days
6. Have team photos
7. Encourage charity
8. Encourage volunteering
9. Raise salaries
10. Remind employees your organisation's mission and values
11. Recognize and encourage innovation
12. Celebrate achievements
13. Celebrate employees
14. Give and receive feedback
15. Try some unusual employee engagement ideas
16. Show respect
17. Empower your employees
18. Support enthusiasm in the workplace
19. Encourage learning
20. Get social
21. Make sure that employees have all the resources they need
22. Seek advice from experts who really know employee engagement
23. Get answers from your employees as well
24. Build long-term engagement

Employee engagement

(Shuck and Wollard, 2010, p. 103) referred Employee engagement as employee's cognitive & emotional attitude toward their organizational performance.

Robinson et al. (2004, p. 9) defined employee engagement as, positivity employees have towards their organisation and its value system. Engaged employees understand organisation goals and align own and their teams efforts towards achieving same.

Towers Perrin (2008) defined employee engagement as the extra time, brainpower, and energy that employees put towards their work that results in discretionary effort.

Right Management (2006) stated that employee engagement is state of employees response to organisational goals having understood its business plan.

Macey et al. (2009) referred employee engagement as visible approach of employees efforts to understand business goals, own role and direct own & team's efforts through initiative and dedication towards organisational goals.

Gallup's Human Sigma website (2005) quoted employee engagement as employees' confidence, integrity and passion directed towards customer satisfaction.

Wellins and Concelman (2004) referred employee engagement as hidden energy which drive employees mentally and physically to play active & committed role to improved productivity, profitability and customer satisfaction using their loyalty, emotional bond and feeling of ownership to the organisational goals.

The Business Communicator (2005) stated 03 definitions of engagement extracted from 03 actively engaged employees as follows:

1. Two well known dimensions of Employee Engagement are job knowledge for understanding role & performing it and motivation to put feeling of achieving organisational goals into action.

2. Employee Engagement enhances employees' commitment levels to become significant contributor to organisational results.

3. Employee engagement is social process transforming employee's into emotionally bonded and significant contributor in the organisational outcomes.

Job satisfaction

(Spector, 1997) termed Job satisfaction as level of positivity employees have for their job roles. Hence in general it can be said that Job Satisfaction is level of happiness of an employee at professional and mental level.

Authors (Igbaria & Buimaraes, 1993) stated that Job satisfaction as basic response of employee in the form of his attitude towards organisation in return of his experience at job role and work place.

Churchill et al. (1974) stated that Job Satisfaction is resultant of job related issues contribution in happiness felt by the employees; drivers for job satisfaction are conduct of immediate manager, pay & allowances, team culture, career development opportunities.

Paul Spector's defined job satisfaction positivity induced by few elements e.g Compensation, Career growth opportunities, immediate manager's conduct, Fringe benefits, rewards & recognition SOP, Team spirit, job role clarity and internal communication.

Well-being

The clinical perspective describes absence of negative conditions as well-being and psychological perspective describes prevalence of positive attributes as well-being.

Angner (2008) stated that, even the philosophical literature refers well-being in variety of ways, which includes Individual's good, welfare, happiness, flourishing, benefit, advantage, interest, sensible value, eudaimonia, usefulness, quality of life, and flourishing.

Seedhouse (1995: 65) defined well-being's 03 sides as, an empty notion, key factor which relates to its meaning, resultant meaning and impact of which is variable as per situation.

(McAllister 2005; Camfield, Streuli, & Woodhead, 2010) stated that well-being as non-appearance of sickness subjectively/objectively, over all happiness in life and can be observed at individual or group level.

Shin & Johnson (1978) referred well-being as happiness from the life style that one can afford and feels appropriate on his scale of happiness.

Subjective Well-Being (SWB)

Deiner (2009) defined "Subjective Well-Being" as analysis of life style of individual's and divided into 03 categories i.e. Happiness from over all life, positivity emanated from feel good sentiments, presence of negative feelings at low count.

(Bradshaw et al. 2007) expressed well-being as over all happiness induced by creating equilibrium of various related factors, evolving resources and managing stress.

Psychological well-being

Psychological wellbeing can be defined by putting few elements together e.g. chase for well-being; compact of qualities; happiness in over all life cycle; socially admirable conduct; manifold magnitudes; and individual positivity.

Organisation culture

The authors suggested that Organisational culture is the values system of an organisation and how it embodies its employees in it convincingly and motivates them to work for the organisational goals. (Enz, 1988; safold 1988)

The author defined that organisation culture is set of certain key or pivotal value system concerning organisational behaviour and state of affairs shared/practised across its branches/units as central vale system. (weiner 1988:535)

The authors referred that an organisation with sustained superior organisational performance is sure to have set of strong core managerial values which the way business and related activities are to be conducted (Deal & Kennedy. 1982; Peters & Waterman, 1982; Trichy, 1983)

Deshpande & Webster (1989, p) defined Organisational culture is spectrum of organisational values & beliefs that are used across the organisation helps employee to comprehend how organisations operate and apprise them about guidelines around which they need to conduct while working in organisation.

Organisation performance

Authors suggested that the organisational performance is resultant of productivity, quality and profitability through well trained, motivated & engaged employees having credible market position (Arthur, 1994; Bailey, 1993; Cutcher-Gershenfeld, 1991; Huselid, 1995)

Authors refer to the organisational performance as output of sustained & collective performance of all the teams placing organisation with competitive edge over rival organisation, giving organisation a long term growth path (Baird & Meshoulam, 1988; Lengnick-Hall & Lengnick-Hall, 1988)

Authors define organisational performance as resultant of Financial performance, Operational performance and organisational effectiveness (Ginsberg,1984; Snow & Hambrick, 1980)

4.6.5.2 Variable factors for the Study

Based on Qualitative Research e.g. Literature survey, Book reviews, Interactions etc following Dependant and Independent variables have been drawn:

Independent variables	Dependent variables
❖ Physical work environment	❖ Job satisfaction
❖ Work life balance	❖ Job involvement
❖ Psychological well-being	❖ Sense of accomplishment
❖ Autonomy	❖ Well-being of employees
❖ Relationship with co-employees and senior management.	❖ Individual performance
❖ Medical facilities given to employees and their family	❖ Organization performance
❖ Canteen facilities provided	
❖ Training and development	
❖ Career opportunities	
❖ Rewards and recognition	
❖ Pay and benefits	
❖ Senior leadership	
❖ Co-employees, team work	

CHAPTER 5

CONCEPTUALISATION OF MODEL (PRE RESEARCH) AND DATA ANALYSIS

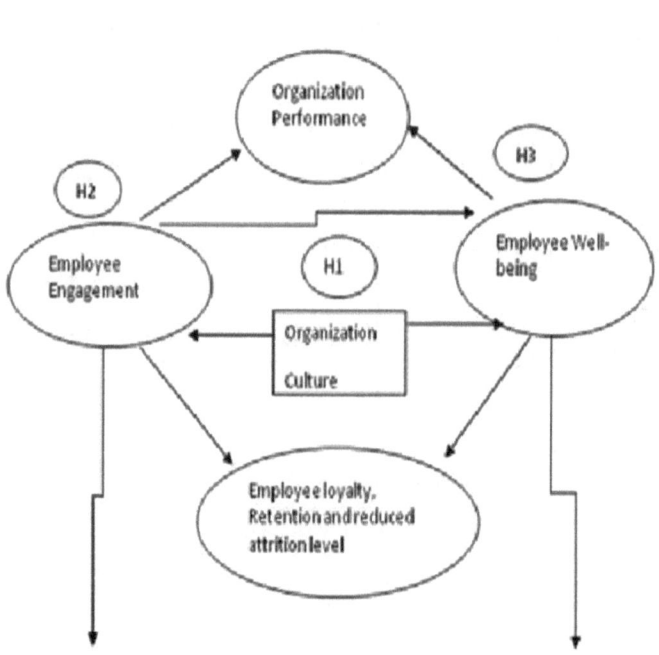

- Job satisfaction
- Job involvement
- Sense of accomplishment
- Training and development
- Career opportunities
- Rewards and recognition
- Pay and benefits
- Senior leadership
- Co-employees, teamwork

- Physical work environment
- Work life balance
- Psychological well-being
- Autonomy
- Relationship with co-employees and senior management.
- Medical facilities given to employees and their family
- Canteen facilities provided
- Financial facilities given for employee welfare.

Figure 15: Conceptualization of Model (Pre Research)

Based on various assumptions and independent & dependent variables following **"Conceptual Model"** was drawn to undertake the study systematically.

DATA ANALYSIS

Table 1: White collared employees experience in the Organization

Work experience in Organization	Frequency	Percentage
0-1 yr	138	23.0
1-2 yrs	121	20.2
2-3 yrs	110	18.3
3-4 yrs	39	6.5
More than 4 yrs	192	32.0
Total	600	100.0

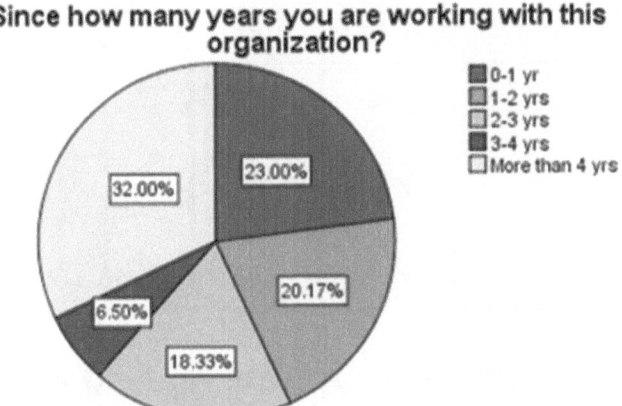

Since how many years you are working with this organization?

Figure 16: Since how many years you are working with the organization? (WCE)

Impacts, reasons of loyalty of white coloured employees for any organisation is different from coloured employee hence response of white coloured employees was collected separately. Few key reasons for white coloured employees working for long term with organisations are Pay & allowances, welfare facilities, Training & Development opportunities, perks and privileges for the designation held by the employee, transparent performance appraisal system, regular increments, promotions' etc.

When we look at the mean experience of blue collared employees in the Organization it is 6 years to 10 years i.e. nearly 69.5% employees are working in the same Organization for minimum 6 years in same Organization. This is important to notice that the employees tend to remain in same Organisation for most of the time of their work tenure as the work allotted to them is specific and they are trained to it perfectly with the given time period and so they are happy, satisfied and loyal to the Organization. Out of 600 employees 533 employees i.e. 88.8% employees have prior work experience. A mean and median year of prior work is 6 to 10 years.

Table 2: Blue collared employees experience in the Organization

Work experience in the Organization	Frequency	Percent
0 - 5 yrs	137	22.8
6 - 10 yrs	417	69.5
11 - 15 yrs	25	4.2
More than 15 yrs	21	3.5
Total	600	100.0

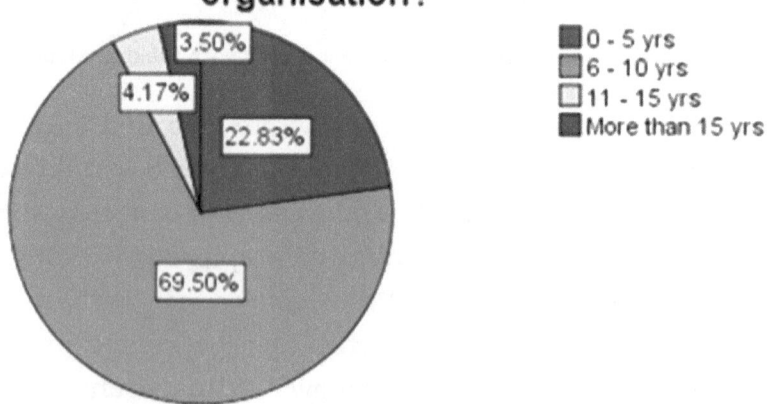

Figure 17: Since how many years you are working with the organization? (BCE)

When it comes to issue of blue coloured employees working for long term with the organisation the deciding factors are different form white coloured employees. Blue coloured employees mostly look for work place closer to their residence or a work place where transportation is provided for travel or company provides accommodation nearby place or within factory compound. Along with nearby living place also are concerned that affordable education facilities nearby, medical health and entertainment facilities in nearby area.

The blue coloured employees wants that company must provide canteen facility which must facilitate meals, tea & snacks during all the shifts either free or highly discounted prices.

Belonging to very conservative family background blue coloured employees have great faith on god & almighty and hence expect a temple in the factory compound. Similarly they also expect celebration of various religious events/festivals.

As blue coloured employee's wages are very low they prefer to work extra i.e. more than 8 hours so that they can earn overtime which is paid @ twice the hourly rate. Similarly, there motivation & engagement also enhance if they are paid various incentives e.g production incentive and attendance incentives which they feel that benefits the organisation hence they must also get share in the benefit for their extra dedication.

When blue coloured employees were asked the question "Since how many years you are working with the organization?" it is seen that highest 69% of employee worked for 6–10 yrs with the organisation. 22.8% employees worked only for 0–5 yrs with the organisation for long term.

Blue coloured employees worked more than 10 yrs with the organisation are only 7.7% due to new opportunities and better salary as they feel that earn experience give them better salaries in other organisations, while other facilities remain almost similar across the industry.

Organisation point of view only 7.7% employees with experience above 11 yrs donot continue for long term hence a negligible factor for the organisation and donot fall in category of alarming attrition rate. This also means that the organisations surveyed have been maintaining high level of employee satisfaction & engagement for more than 90% employees.

Study of employee engagement and well-being levels of organisation and how it impacted the organization performance.

Most Organisations assume that employee engagement has impact on employees well-being which ultimately make employee joined engaged employee's lot. Organisations conduct regular surveys to receive feed backs from employees through internal sources and also external consultants to make/correct/rejig employee engagement strategies.

As there have not been many researches on employee engagement and well-being which can guide the management/ HR managers as to deal with one of the biggest organisational challenges and also most critical organisational objectives.

As HR managers alongwith the top management have been under constant pressures to mitigate this unknown challenge, in their pursuits they have been hunting for some new engagement policy and tried to implement it their organisation. There are cases wherein while implementing adapted engagement policies when HR managers and Management found few of these to be not financially viable, they implemented partially.

Further, the questionnaire was designed in various parts to study the employee engagement and wellbeing of the employees and how it impacted the organization performance. The main objective is to study the well-being through employee engagement of an organization. Let us study all the factors one by one.

1. Organization leadership and planning

It has been found in many researches on organisational performance that even if organisation has best of the plant & machinery and even dedicated employees, it is the organisation's leadership team which play vital role in success of the organisation in terms of performance and growth (with any prejudice to the contribution of Employees and Plant & Machinery).

Various researches on Leadership style have observed that there is "No Right style of Leadership". There is "No Universal style of Leadership". Suitability of Leadership style varies from situation to situation i.e Organisational environment in terms of challenges being faced by organisation, generation of employees to the technology development; working environment, organisational culture etc.

One may find following types of Organisational environment and Leadership Styles:

Organisational environment

a. Stable Environment

b. High growth or changing environment

c. Environment in crisis.

Leadership Styles

a. Participative Leadership

b. Declarative Leadership

c. Authoritarian Leadership

Class of employees

a. In-experienced Subordinates

b. Capable Subordinates

c. Expert Subordinates

Leadership Styles Grid

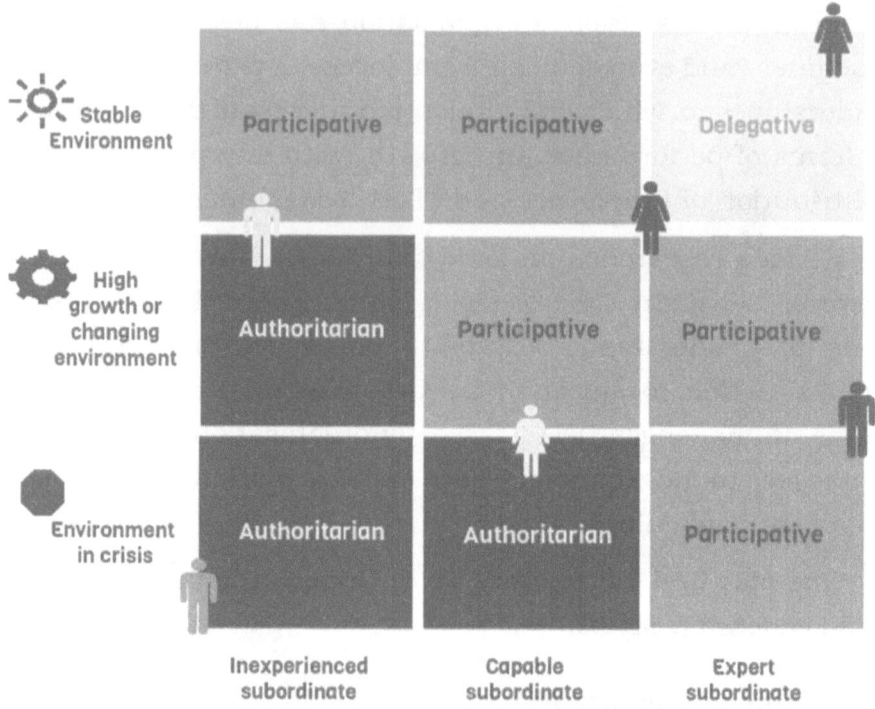

Figure 18: Leadership Style Grid

Organization and To find out the organization leadership and how much employees are aware of the organization we formulated few questions which were asked to both white collared and blue collared employees. They were asked whether they are satisfied with their leadership and are their aware of goals and objectives of the organization. This is important to know that how much employees are aware of the organization and how much they believe in organization. This depicts the open culture of organization which helps employees to live freely in organization while working on their goals. Their goals should match with the organization goal as it will help employees to fulfil their goal which ultimately fulfils organization goal.

When asked to white collared employees, out of 600 employees 80.8% employees feel satisfied while working with the organization and in case of blue collared employees 77.8% employees feel satisfied. Feeling satisfied while working for the organization is important because it indicates the employees' basic needs are getting fulfilled and he is happy with the rules and regulations and the policies of the organization.

When asked the employees about their goals and objectives, only 41% of the white collared employees know the organization goals and objective while nearly 59% does not know about it. This questions was specifically asked to white collared employees only as they are engaged mostly in office/desk work and the hierarchy is mostly well defined in the organizations and so every employee is told his key areas of responsibilities which are in alignment with the organization goal. Again it shows how an employee is engaged in Organisation goal with his/her personal goal. But unfortunately only 41% employees know the organization goal.

The next question was asked about the leadership in organization, whether employees trust their leadership and do the leaders live the core value of organization. This is important question from the organization point of view as it depicts the leadership is well managed and widely accepted by all the employees and they are happy with their senior leaders and would like to work under them and would like to refer the leaders as their role model. It not only will increase their efficiency but also their trust level towards leaders and organization too. Ultimately it will result in healthy relationship between Leaders and employees and will help in maintaining the wellbeing of employees, i.e. psychological well-being. It will ultimately result in increase in organization performance. Nearly 75% of blue collared employees have confidence in their organization leaders while

Blue collared employees

Table 3: Are you satisfied with the Organization? (BCE)

Options	No. of employees	Percent
Yes	470	78.3
No	130	21.7
Total	600	100.0

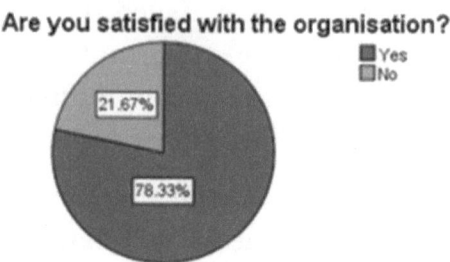

Figure 19: Are you satisfied with the Organization? (BCE)

Though satisfaction of all the stake holders is key factor for organisational success and growth. Blue coloured employees are the one who perform under the extreme working conditions and that too for low salaries just because they come from low strata of the society having poorly educated and have no option than to work in same city due to relocation is just not viable.

Keeping in view their crucial role satisfaction levels of such employees is very critical for any organisation as not only they do manual work but they are also mostly united work force when it comes to management decision on their wages, perks & privileges, service conditions as by getting united they are able to do collective negotiations and also protect their jobs while in case of management (white coloured) employees collection bargaining is not permitted by the management, they are ruled by HR policies which is applicable across this category of employees.

It is seen that nearly 78% of the blue collared employees are happy with the organization while rest are unhappy.

Table 4: Do you have confidence in leadership? (BCE)

Options	No. of employees	Percentage
Yes	453	75.5
No	147	24.5
Total	600	100.0

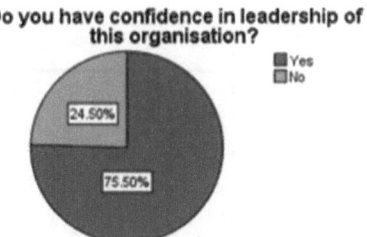

Figure 20: Do you have confidence in leadership? (BCE)

Productivity of employees especially blue coloured employees is not a mechanical system which works by a Switch ON/OFF way. They are the people who have to deal with many masters such as supervisor, foreman, plant head, SBU head, Top Management etc directly/indirectly along with handling their own personal & professional challenges which are generally unavoidable.

In order to have absolute labour peace and blue coloured employees expect that their leaders conduct and treat them fairly & with equality so that there in rift among their class of employees for simple reason that if the leaders engage them with disparity they will not be able to work as team member emotionally, mentally and professionally.

Nearly 75.5% employees have confidence in leadership so we can assume that they can work happily in the organization.

Table 5: Do you think that leaders in this Organization are ready to accept inputs from employees? (BCE)

Scale	No. of employees	Percent
Very often	244	40.7
Often	189	31.5
Sometimes	114	19.0
Rarely	43	7.2
Never	10	1.7
Total	600	100.0

Figure 21: Do you think that leaders in this Organization are ready to accept inputs from employees? (BCE)

Though production targets of an organisation largely depend upon out put of blue coloured employees but when it is matter of organisational performance, growth and decision making Top management have to play diligent & timely role to set direction of organisational performance strategy and growth over short and long period.

Scientifically, numbers speaks for itself in terms of performance & growth but whether the numbers set as target and achieved and the manner these were achieved go in long way for any growing organisation. To set these goals right and guiding the team and facilitate right training blue coloured employees are required to be led by superiors who are supposed to take the whole team through the task. If the superiors donot take initiative and lead in time a well-crafted growth plan also fails miserably.

Nearly 40% say very often while 31% say often that leaders in the organization are ready to accept the inputs. So in most of the organizations seniors accept the input from employees.

Table 6: Do you think senior leaders live the core value of the organisation ? (BCE)

Options	No. of employees	Percentage
Yes	453	75.5
No	147	24.5
Total	600	100.0

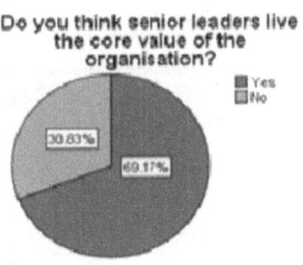

**Figure 22: Do you think senior leaders live the core value
of the organisation? (BCE)**

Core values of an organisation play vital role in creating culture of the organisation in terms of its reputation, building new generation and socially responsible entity and global player.

Most organisations during their growth path set core value as management styles, but it takes long time for it imbibe it in actual across the organisation as for this functioning of the organisation need radical changes so as its top management's working style as cultural change flows top to bottom.

In doing so many organisations commence inculcating core values in the form of pledge by employees, declaration/ commitment by the employees and also few sermons by top management to middle & junior staff.

Core values are needed to be owned and respected by top management & executives of leadership position, first they need to exhibit their respect & compliance for the core value that sends message for all to abide by it.

Nearly 70% employees agree to it that their leaders live the core value and so they can act as a role model for others.

Table 7: Do you have clear understanding of your job role ? (BCE)

options	No. of employees	Percentage
Yes	336	56.0
No	264	44.0
Total	600	100.0

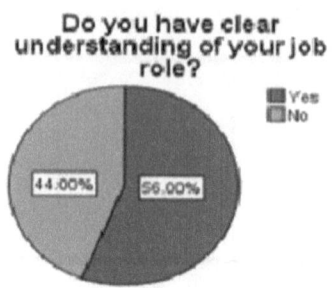

Figure 23: Do you have clear understanding of your job role? (BCE)

Only 56% of the employees have clear understanding of their job while 44% does not have it. It is important to tell them their job role in detail. **White collared employees**

Table 8: Are you satisfied with the organization?(WCE)

option	No. of employees	Percentage
Yes	485	80.8
No	115	19.2
Total	600	100.0

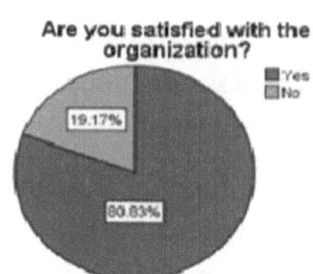

Figure 24: Are you satisfied with the organization? (WCE)

Nearly 80% white collared employees are satisfied with the organization.

Table 9: Are you aware of the goals and objectives of the organization?(WCE)

Option	No. of employees	Percentage
Yes	249	41.5
No	351	58.5
Total	600	100.0

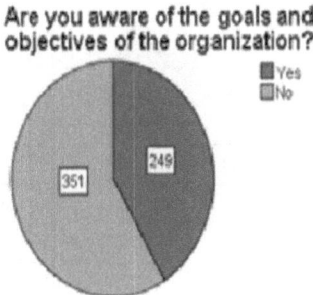

Figure 25: Are you aware of the goals and objectives of the organization?(WCE)

Only 41% employees know about the organization goal. It is very important and can be of concern as individual goal is derived from organization goal.

Table 10: Do you have confidence in leadership of this Organization(WCE)

option	No. of employees	Percentage
Yes	554	92.3
No	46	7.7
Total	600	100.0

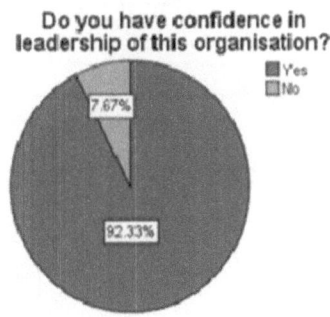

Figure 26: Do you have confidence in leadership of this Organization (WCE)

Nearly 92% employees have confidence in leadership and it is a positive factor.

Table 11: Rating of confidence in leadership on the given scale.(WCE)

Ratings	No. Of employees	Percentage
Lowest	13	2.32
Low	40	7.15
Neutral	169	30.23
High	240	42.93
Highest	97	17.35
Total	559	100

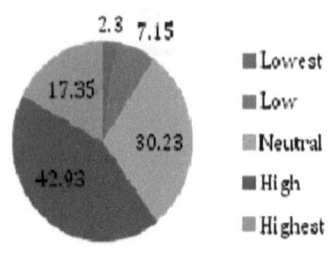

Figure 27: Rating of confidence in leadership on the given scale.(WCE)

When asked about give rating of confidence in leadership, 17.35% and 42.93% confided in Leadership as Highest and High respectively. 30% remained neutral while 10% approx. gave negative.

Table 12: Do you think senior leaders live the core value of the Organization?(WCE)

Option	No. of employees	Percentage
Yes	524	87.3
No	76	12.7
Total	600	100.0

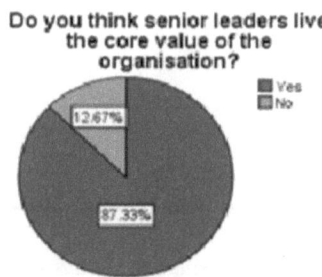

Figure 28: Do you think senior leaders live the core value of the Organization? (WCE)

Nearly 87% employees think that their managers live the core value of organization

Table 13: Rating on the given scale (WCE)

Ratings	No. Of employees	Percentage
Lowest	16	3
Low	43	8.08
Neutral	190	35.71
High	185	34.77
Highest	98	18.42
Total	532	100

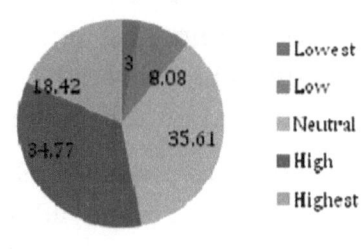

Figure 29: Rating on the given scale (WCE)

Table 14: Do you think that leaders in this Organization are ready to accept inputs from employees?(WCE)

Options	No. of employees	Percentage
Yes	502	83.7
No	98	16.3
Total	600	100.0

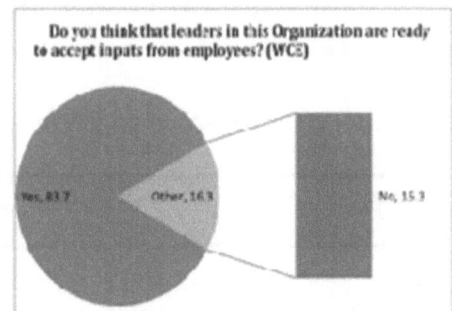

Figure 30: Do you think that leaders in this Organization are ready to accept inputs from employees? (WCE)

In pre 1970 era, it was only promoters who used to take all the decisions and employees expected to only do what was told to do irrespective of their qualification, experience etc.

Times have changed and involvement of employees in troubleshooting and decision making. Now a days Departments, SBU, Divisions are led by professionals and even Management board has employees as members unlike earlier when only family members used to be members of board.

With introduction of Best practices like ISO, 5S, TPM, TQM, Six Sigma, SA-8000 etc in the business and its increasing dominance has increased role of employees as leaders/members of troubleshooting teams, management committees etc. Such initiatives have brought remarkable change in the organisational culture and performance.

Apart from above, Employee suggestions scheme, KAIZEN etc initiatives have added many new process improvements, waste controls, time savings etc.

When white coloured employees where asked Question "Do you think that leaders in this Organization are ready to accept inputs from employees?" Nearly 83% of employees think that managers are ready to accept the inputs from employees. Which clearly indicate that most organisations have gone through significant cultural change over the period and give value to employee's inputs for benefit of the organisation.

Table 15: Is the Organization internal communication detailed enough? (WCE)

Options	No. of employees	Percentage
Yes	512	85.3
No	88	14.7
Total	600	100.0

Figure 31: Is the Organization internal communication detailed enough?(WCE)

One of the pioneer assumed tool to engage employees was direct communication with the employees. This is one tool which has gone through serial changes that started from periodic messages to the employees in form of Diwali wishes etc, which moves further in the form of "from chairman's desk". Once organisations realised its importance it moved further in the direct communication with employee. Now most organisations have exclusive mail box to communicate with employees which have grown to the level where in top management share key decisions, policy change, merger, de merger and new acquisitions and even share major financial decisions.

Many organisations have also introduced weekly/monthly internal magazines which not only share operations, business update of the organisations but also print pictures of star performers, information on various events held in group company's units and even the pictures and details of events at residence of employees. Even such magazines, mails boxes share creative works of employees and even their family members e.g. poetry, sketches, photo flicks etc. Hence, it is assumed by most organisation that open and detailed communications between management and employees is need of every organisation to build pool of actively engaged employee through two way communication on any issue pertaining to operations, business, cultural, welfare or even awareness.

Nearly 85% of employees think that there is open and detailed communication in the organization which is important factor of employee engagement. This indicate that open and detailed communication with employee has great bearing on the relationship between top management and employees.

Table 16: Ratings in the given scale (WCE)

Ratings	No. Of employees	Percentage
Lowest	137	26.86275
Low	191	37.45098
Neutral	22	4.313725
High	150	29.41176
Highest	10	1.960784
Total	510	100

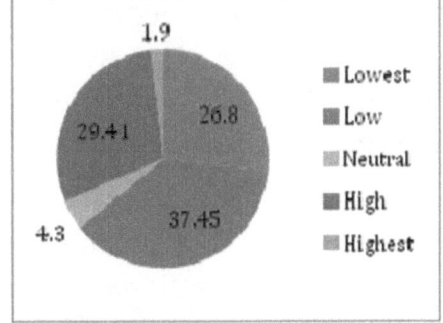

Figure 32: Ratings in the given scale (WCE)

Office Equipments

Till late 1980s, for preparing any document Type writers were the only solution till they started phasing out in early 1990s and electronic type writers were newly entered the market which were merely better version of type writer with editing and also electronic printing facility. When in 1990s Computers with word star software entered it was a revolutionary change in the typing & documenting, recording data etc.

Between 1990 and 1999 computer technology gone through remarkable evolutions from MS-DOS to word star 5, word star 7, Lotus and by 1995 Windows 95, 97 came and world came under panic when with the turn of century problem Y2K hit all the computers which was sorted out by Microsoft by launching VISTA, Windows 2000, 2010 etc.

The point which is driven from this above evolution is that computers and printing mechanism have brought great revolution in office functioning, to the extent that employees link PC configuration, Laptop, type of printers status symbol the position held by them and they expect such office equipment as minimum operational need.

This operational need started from basic cell phone and as on date even a junior executive feels need for Black Berry and seniors' iPhones to use various office Apps, accessing mails and even downloading attachments of large files to respond/take action. This has virtually filled the "Zone time gap" among the countries for functioning and executives can interact with their counter parts across the world 24x7.

In 1990s, cell phone communication was very costly and there were no Apps available to make executives easier, but as of now communications is very cheap & affordable but there are many interactive Apps for voice/data/video communications which free to use such as WhatsApp, Viber, Line, Face-time,

WeChat, FB, Twitter, Linkedin. Hence, Communication has become vital part of functioning/performance.

Table 17: Do you get all the required office equipment needed for your role at your work place? (WCE)

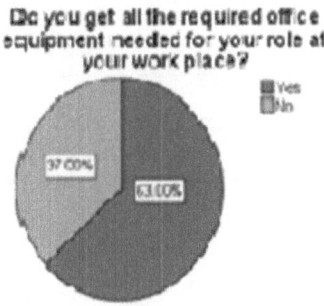

Option	No. of employees	Percentage
Yes	378	63.0
No	222	37.0
Total	600	100.0

Figure 33: Do you get all the required office equipment needed for your role at your work place? (WCE)

When employees were asked question "Do you get all the required office equipment needed for your role at your work place?" from white coloured employees, 63% employees responded positively and said that they have been given appropriate office equipments necessary to perform the task/role.

Combined results

Table 18: Are you satisfied with the Organization?

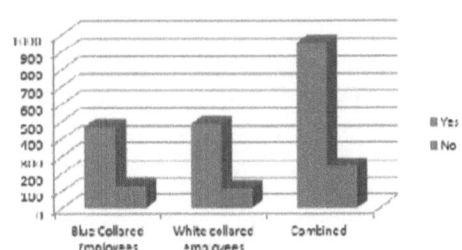

Option	Blue Collared Employees	White collared employees	Combined	Percentage
Yes	470	485	955	79.5833333
No	130	115	245	20.4166667
Total	600	600	1200	300

Figure 34: Are you satisfied with the Organization?

Nearly 80% of both employees are happy with organization which shows that they like the organization and so the job too.

Table 19: Do you have confidence in leadership?

Option	Blue Collared Employees	White collared employees	Combined	Percentage
Yes	453	554	1007	83.9166667
No	147	46	193	16.0833333
Total	600	600	1200	100

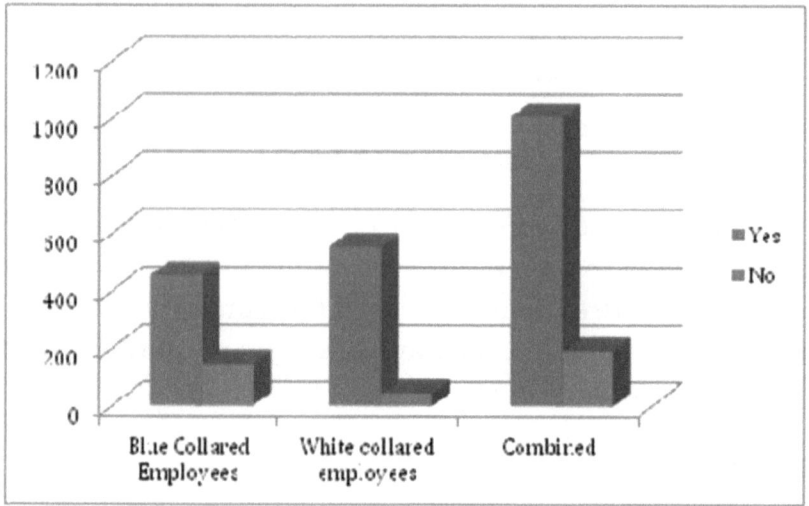

Figure 35: Do you have confidence in leadership?

Nearly 84% employees have confidence in the leadership of organization. So they can see their leader as a guide and mentor to improve in their work and trust them for what they are saying.

Table 20: Do you think senior leaders live the core value of the Organization?

Option	Blue Collared Employees	White collared employees	Combined	Percentage
Yes	415	524	939	85.3636364
No	85	76	161	14.6363636
Total	600	600	1100	100

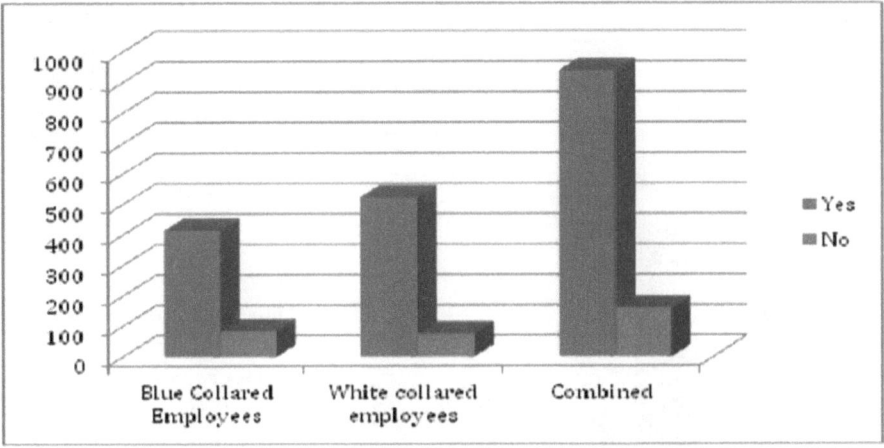

Figure 36. Do you think senior leaders live the core value of the Organization?

Nearly 85% employees think the leaders live the core value of the organization. So they practice what they say. It helps in increasing the confidence of employees in the leaders.

Table 21: Do you think that leaders in this Organization are ready to accept inputs from employees?

Option	Blue Collared Employees	White collared employees	Combined	Percentage
Very often	244	153	397	33.0833333
Often	189	183	372	31
Sometimes	114	27	141	11.75
Rarely	43	126	169	14.0833333
Never	10	111	121	10.0833333
Total	600	600	1200	100

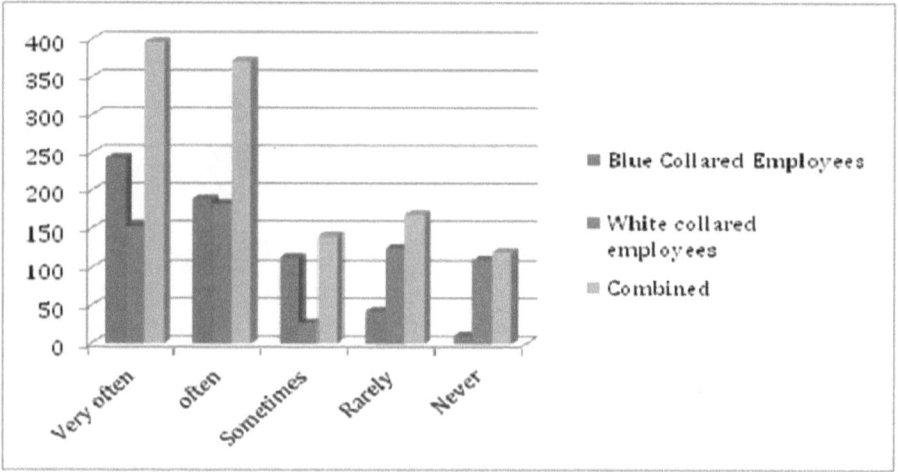

Figure 37: Do you think that leaders in this Organization are ready to accept inputs from employees?

When the employees are given freedom to take decision for their work, they not only feel empowered but also involve in the task in detail and use their full potential to complete the given task. Giving them platform to express their ideas or accepting their inputs for improvement of work not only give them recognition (Social need- Maslow's Hierarchy of needs) but also increase their confident (self-esteem – Maslow's hierarchy of needs). When these needs are fulfilled employees are bound to engage at the workplace and use their optimum potential to complete their task.

The communication in the organization plays a prime role in employee engagement and employee well-being. The transparent vertical communication is very important as it will reduce the gaps between senior management and employees. So employees can approach senior management for their issues resolution and for getting guidance to achieve their goals. It not only keeps them happy and involved in the work they do but also psychologically satisfied and content for their work.

2. Organization culture and work environment

Organisation culture refers to the working style of leadership & management which set the direction of the ethical & moral ratings and goals of the organisation as to what is ethical & morally correct and acceptable in the organisation and what is prohibited.

Many researchers have quoted in their researches that it is the leaders and management who need to set the example to their work force what they expect them to conduct, perform and what is not expected and acceptable. Organizational culture is created by the attitude, approach and modes adopted by the management & leaders while dealing with customers, employees, own conduct and also even duty to nation in terms of compliance to statutory regulations.

Organisational culture also deals with the level of transparency in executing transactions abiding by law, accounting standards, documentations, clarity in setting organisational goals, leaders goals, internal controls & audits and business & employee performance evaluation systems. These measures build confidence among organisation, customers, govt authorities, employees about the management that there is nothing which being violated and done in clandestine manner. These practise create a bond of confidence among them help build a well-knit team for a larger morally & ethical organisational objectives.

Types of organisational cultures

There are various types of organisational cultures in vogue across the industry. However, broadly organisational culture can be categorised in in two dimensions as under:

Strategic dimension

These types of organisations have been defined & separated from each other based on adaptive nature/orientation of an organisation:

a. Clan oriented: Such organisations believe in working as well knit teams on personal & professional levels. In such organisations hand holding is one of the way of performing, mentoring, nurturing and grooming the future generations to ensure that organisation's working style remains unchanged if not better so as to ensure stable organisational performance. These organisations are also some times termed as "Family cultured organisations"

b. Adhocracy oriented: Such organisations believe in cultures of doing taking up new challenges, new business opportunities, innovations', new learnings. Such organisations allow and motivate employees to explore new opportunities and take new risks for growth of organisation for profitability and foe self-career development as professional as well.

c. Market oriented: Such organisations believe in matching with the market needs and getting edge over competitors, being marker leaders and focus on achieving organisational goals by meeting market goals & competitions. This type of culture puts through teams under newer challenges & pressures very frequently which need team to really think out of box to meet the challenges.

d. Hierarchy oriented: Such organisations are defined as most professional organisations which are managed through systems & processes than particular person. These have well defined hierarchy clearly stating channel of communications, chart of authority with accountability.

These organisations believe in adopting Best Practices and have virtually Zero tolerance for errors and wastages for efficiency and stability.

There is no right or wrong Organisational culture, it depends upon the stage of maturity of the organisation, its management, employees and the challenges faced by the organisation, vision of the organisation to "go global"

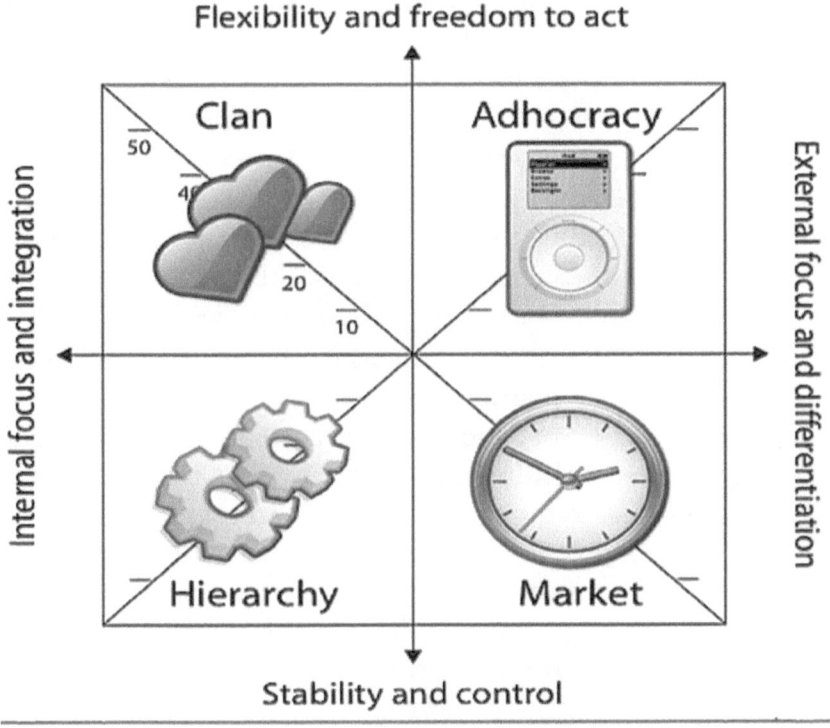

Figure 38: Organisational Culture Grid

Behavioural dimension

Organisational culture is basically package of customs, attitudes, and beliefs that separate each organisation from others and so the success and growth graph. As culture is a process some organisations adapt the cultures quickly some take little longer. Some organisations go through autonomous change accept it as need for sustenance while some take its mid path of either slow change or some take tougher path of changing even leadership roles down to key roles for the single bottom line to success and that is "organisational need"

There broadly nine types of Organisational cultures as under:

a. Academy culture: Such organisations are very particular about selectin of employees based on qualification and emphasis greatly on training & development of employee. Such organisations also make great efforts to retain the employees and promote innovations and new developments. Examples: Hospitals, Educational bodies etc

b. Pragmatic culture: "Customer is king of the market" is the guiding and ruling factor of such organisations making them very flexible and changing as per market needs and in tern make them very successful and fastest growing organisations. Examples: FMCG, Service industry etc

c. Club culture: Such organisations are into niche industry where in qualification comes first, followed by specific experience, error free track record of candidate before they are even called for interview. Such organisations need continuous improving training and performance evaluation process to meet frequently (termed as daily changing) market needs. However, such organisations pay their employees well for the high quality rated performance and also frequent promotions. Example: Airlines, Intelligence services etc.

d. Normative culture: Such organisations are also called "by the book entities" means that they have very strict work procedures and compliance expectations. Working in such organisation is very difficult unless one is very disciplined and donot have problems in working without autonomy and flexibility at work. Example: Defence forces, Govt Organisations etc

e. Baseball culture: Such organisations are design, evolve and modify their culture as per the employees needs as they believe that "Employee is key for the organisational success" as long as employees are happy, motivated and engaged we will lead the market as engaged employees perform best for the organisations goal & growth. Example: Google, Nokia, Apple etc

f. Tough guy culture: Such organisations believe in closely & continuously monitoring performance of employees micro managing the process of delivery/performance. These companies have well defined process without any scope of deviations, however, giving space to human errors concepts like "three error escape" system is followed wherein three genuine human errors are pardonable before employee is sacked. Example: call centre etc

g. Fortress culture: Such organisations are highly stressful organisations with the employee point of view as such organisations hire employees in high numbers than needed voluntarily prepared for certain% of attrition to match up with market needs by retaining only performers and dumping non-performers. However, such organisations are really well paying for those who are really good at their job and such employees can be assured of their long term job in an organisation. Example: Retail, Perishable goods etc

h. Process culture: These organisations have well defined process which are just expected that these should be followed to contain failures and wastage unlike normative culture where regulations are like working at gun point. The employees are not either micro managed or closely monitored. Such organisations usually follow yearly performance reviews. Employees work more aligned to ideology than the rule book. Example: PSUs etc

i. Bet your company culture: Such organisations have high risk taking systems and process. The quantum of risks is so high that it can be make or break history by decisions by single, few or a team's risk taking initiatives. However, these organisations believe in lot of research and data analysis which makes the risk taker more confident and accurate in their actions. Example: Share brokering firms etc

The organization culture and work environment at the work place plays a vital role in employee engagement and so the well-being. As it not only affect their physical well-being but the psychological well-being as well.

Work environment is very significant while studying the engagement and well-being as it not only indicates how employees feel safe and secure in the organization

The work place climate in most industries is very unsafe and in pathetic condition due to lack of proper ventilation, improper/insufficient lighting, unsafe drinking water, polluted air due to dust/fumes, high decibel noise, poor state of office structure and equipment provided to employees to execute tasks etc. Further, these organisations despite knowing these organisation lack basic fire & industrial safety equipments/personal safety equipments, emergency services, health services etc. These factors have direct impact on employee's engagement levels and performance as well.

In the recent past there has been a revolutionary change in the approach in the employer's attitude wherein they have started taking these hazards seriously and mitigating with professional approach.

Most organisations now have very motivating policies such as Environment, Health & Safety polices in place with lot of emphasis health & safety of employees while at work place. Apart from these employers have also introduced motivational schemes such as Performance based incentives, Variable pay, flexi timing, maternity & paternity leaves to maintain work life balance etc.

Organisations also have taken initiative to connect with the employees directly through exclusive communication channel sharing organisational information.

To help employees improve their performance and also add up new skills In addition to motivation, employees need the skills and ability to do their job effectively. And for many organisations, training the employee has become a necessary input into the production process.

The next question asked was having a scale of 1 to 7, 1 is being lowest and 7 is being highest. The factors included in this table was related to organization culture, work environment, work in organization. The questions are directly related to the employee engagement and their well-being. These are used to measure the employee engagement in the organization. It is meant to measure the trust level, quality, and cooperation with senior leaders, peers and subordinates.

Table 22: Employee engagement factors I – (Combined)

	Blue collared employees (%)	White collared employees (%)	Combined (%)
Organization Culture			
Trust level of organization.	28.9	14.3	21.6
Quality of product for customer satisfaction.	50.5	50.05	50.5
Co-operation among the seniors peers and subordinates.	64.35	50.05	57.2
Work environment			
Safety measures taken by organization.	35.75	57.20	46.47
Physical working conditions.	57.20	57.20	57.2

Temperature of work place.	64.35	64.35	64.35
Noise control at work place.	64.35	71.5	67.92
Regular inspection of the plant and machinery to avoid the hazards organized by organization.	71.5	71.5	71.5
Are the seniors easily approachable?	71.5	57.20	64.35
Do you have a freedom to express your opinion without any negative consequences?	28.6	57.20	42.9
WORK IN THE ORGANIZATION			
Do you feel that you can trust your supervisor?	42.9	57.20	50.05
Do you like your job ?	71.5	57.20	64.35
Do you think that your job is secure?	71.5	57.20	64.35
How do you rate your present job with the skill set you have?	71.5	71.5	71.5
How will you rate organization's respect and value towards you?	71.5	57.20	64.35

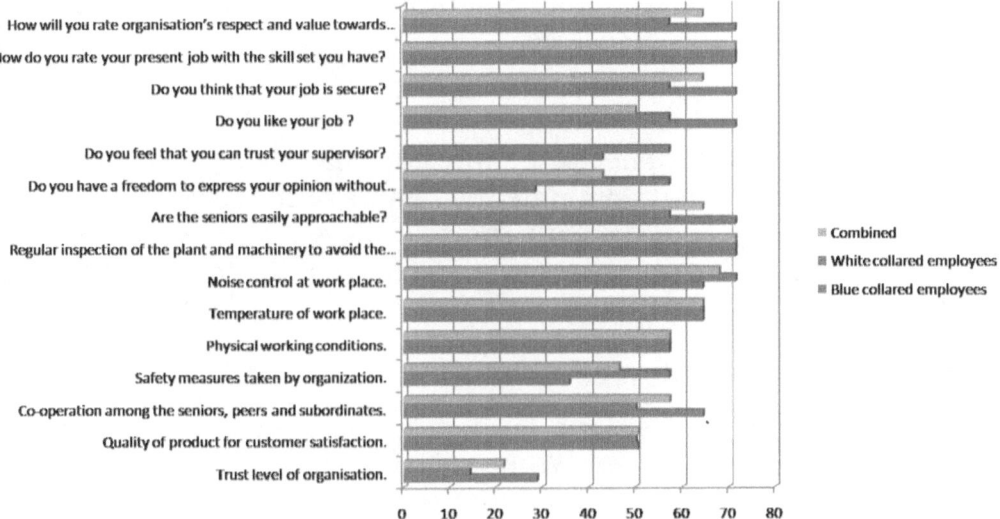

Figure 39: Employee engagement factors -I (Combined)

The factors related to work culture; work environment and the relationship with the employees surrounding you in organization play a crucial role in employee engagement. When asked about Trust level nearly 28.9% Blue collared and 14.3% white collared employees answers affirmatively. Quality of product for customer satisfaction is better is agreed by nearly 50.5% of the employees. Nearly 57.2% of all the employees think there is better co-operation among the seniors, peers and subordinates. About the work environment some questions were asked. The result is shown in figure and the table above. Overall the work environment is properly maintained and they can perform their work comfortably in the environment. Overall 60% employees are happy with the work environment.

Some of the questions were asked about their perception about the job they are doing and their surroundings. 64.35% employees said that their seniors are easily approachable. 42.9% employees said that they have freedom to express their opinion without any negative consequences. 50% employees trust their supervisor, 64.35% employees like their job and feel their job is secure. 71.5% employees think that their job matches with their skills and knowledge so they can complete their job effectively.

64.35% employees feel that organization respect them value them as its effective employee.

Factor analysis

Factor analysis is done to identify the major observed & co-related variables that dominate the results of the research. This analysis clearly brings about the role played by the variables in concluding the objectives of the research as to accepting/ rejecting the hypothesis.

White collared employees

The factor analysis is done to identify the major variables for the employee engagement. When it is done first, the result is as follows,

Table 23: Component Matrix (WCE)

	Component	
	1	2
Trust level of organisation	.702	-.426
Quality of product for customer satisfaction.	.744	-.288
Co-operation among the seniors, peers and subordinates.	.692	-.292
Safety measures taken by organization	.787	-.172
Physical working conditions.	.716	-.280
Temperature of work place	.734	-.053
Noise control at work place.	.707	-.085
Are the seniors easily approachable?	.629	.259
Do you have a freedom to express your opinion without any negative consequences?	.632	.313
Do you feel that you can trust your supervisor?	.710	.025
Do you like your job ?	.722	.271
Do you think that your job is secure?	.682	.097
How do you rate your present job with the skill set you have?	.663	.425
How will you rate organisation's respect and value towards you?	.667	.341

Extraction Method: Principal Component Analysis.

After removing the factors which are rated below 7 are removed from the list and again factor analysis done. The result is as follows,

Table 24: Component Matrix final (WCE)

	Component
	1
Trust level of organisation	.765
Quality of product for customer satisfaction.	.787
Co-operation among the seniors, peers and subordinates.	.735
Safety measures taken by organization.	.821
Physical working conditions.	.756
Temperature of work place.	.744
Noise control at work place.	.714
Do you feel that you can trust your supervisor?	.705

Extraction Method: Principal Component Analysis.

a. 1 components extracted.

The above are the main variables which directly affect the employee engagement for white collared employees.

Factor analysis for blue collared employees

Table 25: Component Matrix (BCE)

	Component		
	1	2	3
Trust level of organisation.	.718	.016	-.087
Quality of product for customer satisfaction.	.627	-.185	.223
Co-operation among the seniors peers and subordinates.	.730	.089	-.226
Safety measures taken by organization	.660	-.330	.322
Physical working conditions.	.588	.340	-.226
Temperature of work place.	.616	-.484	.291
Noise control at work place	.588	.500	-.258
Regular inspection of the plant and machinery to avoid the hazards organised by organization.	.541	-.466	.147
Are the seniors easily approachable?	.597	.435	.145
Do you have a freedom to express your opinion without any negative consequences?	.513	-.467	-.311
Do you feel that you can trust your supervisor?	.495	.421	.472
Do you like your job ?	.496	-.170	-.470
Do you think that your job is secure?	.451	.266	.456
How do you rate your present job with the skill set you have?	.441	.067	-.230
How will you rate organisation's respect and value towards you?	.541	.037	-.240

Ex Traction Method: Principal Component Analysis

a. 3 components extracted.

After removing the factors which are rated below 7 are removed from the list and again factor analysis done. The result is as follows,

Table 26: Component Matrix final (BCE)

	Component
	1
Trust level of organisation	.765
Quality of product for customer satisfaction.	.787
Co-operation among the seniors, peers and subordinates.	.735
Safety measures taken by organization.	.821
Physical working conditions.	.756
Temperature of work place.	.744
Noise control at work place.	.714
Do you feel that you can trust your supervisor?	.705

Extraction Method: Principal Component Analysis.

a. 1 components extracted.

These are the main variables which directly affect the employee engagement for white collared employees.

Table 27: Employee engagement factors II

Sr. No.	Factor	Blue collared employees (%)	White collared employees (%)	Combined Effect(%)
1	Have you been treated well by the managers?	80	80	80
2	Does your supervisor/manager handle your work related issue satisfactorily?	75	75	75
3	Does your supervisor/manager tell when you do your job well?	75	75	75
4	Does your supervisor/manager tell when you need any improvement?	75	75	75
5	Do you like to go to job every day?	75	75	75

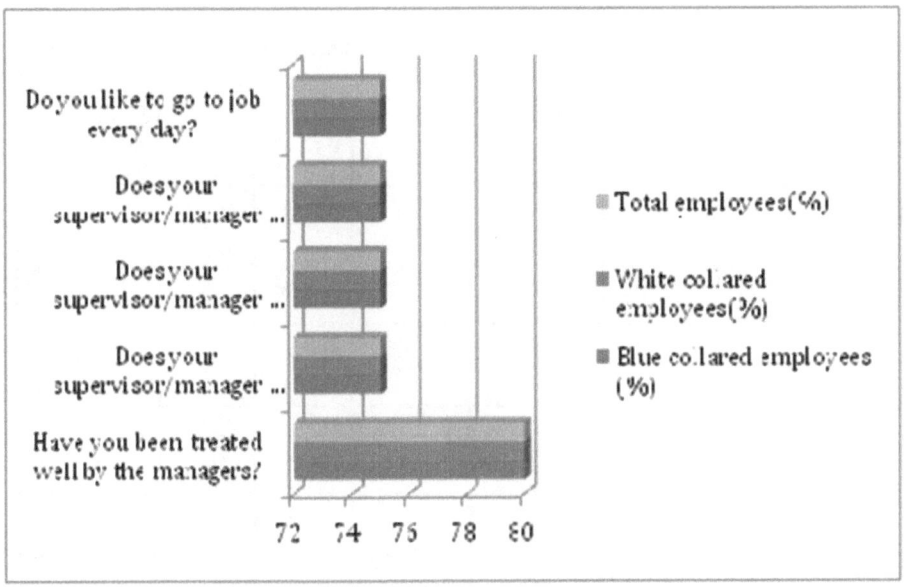

Figure 40: Employee engagement factors II

The above factors indicate that how employees are treated in the organization, by their immediate managers and senior managers. It is directly related to the employee's psychological well-being as it may boost the employee to work better or can have negative impact if he will not get proper treatment by his seniors. As seen above employees are happy working with organisation as they getting treated well by their managers, they are told when they do their job well and when they need improvement in work. So nearly 75% employees like their job and want to go to job every day.

Table 28: Employee engagement factors related to salary and other facilities (Blue collared employees)

Sr. No.	Factor/scale	Excellent (%)	Very good (%)	Good (%)	Fair (%)	Needs improvement (%)
1.	The pay/salary you getting for the work/job.	25.8	23.2	28.3	14	7.7
2.	Amount of leaves you get.	5.7	28.5	37	21	7.8
3.	The overtime pay you get for extra work done	10.2	25.8	37.7	18	8.3
4.	The bonus.	7.7	17.7	39	28	7.7
5.	Canteen facilities of organization.	8	24	32.7	20.2	15
6.	Adequate breaks during work.	5.7	22.7	37.3	25.2	9.7
7.	Any bus facility to commute to work place.	7.7	36.2	38.7	19.5	8
8.	Financial help for children education.	7	22.7	33	28.7	8.7
9.	Medical facilities for you.	7.8	21.7	38.2	25.2	7.2
10.	Medical facilities for your family.	6	19.3	38.8	26.7	9.2
11.	Loan facility for marriage.	4.8	17	40.2	28.5	9.5
12.	Loan facility for building house.	3.5	15.2	38.2	28.3	14.8
13.	Annual family get together for employees.	5.5	17.2	36.5	24.8	16

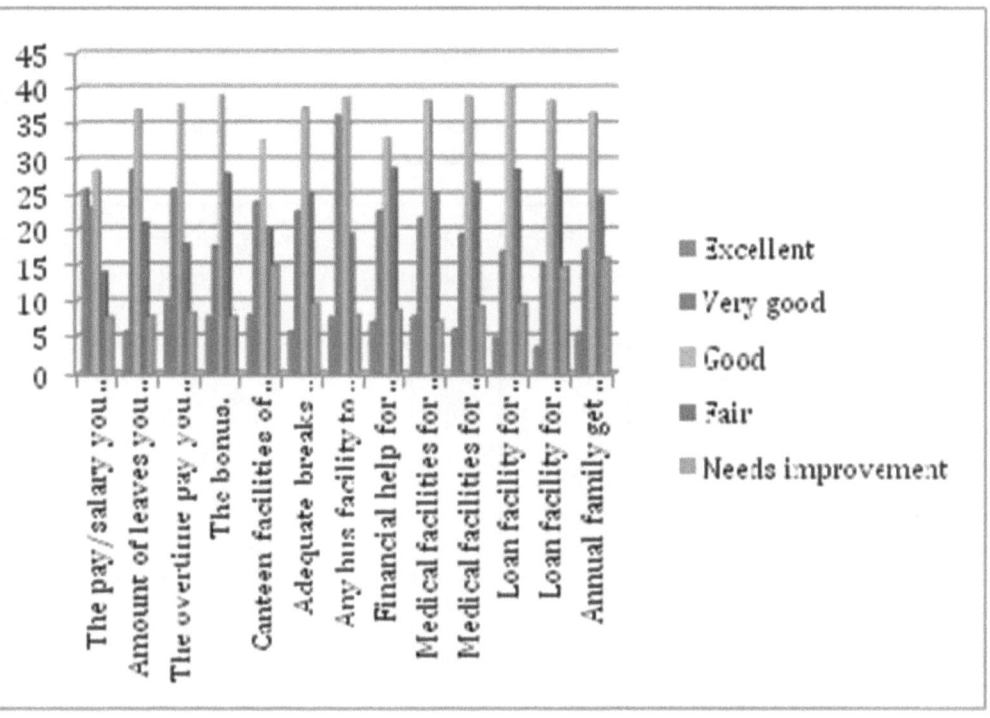

Figure 41: Employee engagement factors related to salary and other facilities (Blue collared employees)

The above mentioned factors are directly related to employee engagement, Pay and other facilities provided by organization to employees. Nearly 26% employees think the salary is excellent while 23% employees feel it is very good. Amount of leaves they are getting yearly are satisfactory for nearly 71% of employees. Nearly 73% employees are happy with the overtime they for extra work done. 65% employees feel that the canteen facilities are good or very good in the organization. 65% employees think the amount of breaks during the working hours is good or better. 62% employees are happy with financial help for child education while 67% are satisfied with the medical facilities for them and 64% employees are happy for the medical facilities for their families. Some of the organizations provide loan facilities to employees, nearly 61% employees like the loan facilities for marriage, 65% are happy with loan facilities for house building. While 58% employees are happy with annual family get together.

Table 29: Employee engagement factors related to salary and other facilities (white collared employees)

Sr. No.	Factor/scale	Excellent (%)	Very good (%)	Good (%)	Fair (%)	Needs improvement (%)
1.	The pay/salary you getting for the work/job.	38.3	28.3	26.5	4.8	1.5
2.	Amount of leaves you get.	11.7	49.7	33.5	5	0.7
3.	Financial help for children education.	15.2	27.7	30.2	17.1	9.3
4.	Medical facilities for you.	10.7	31	43.5	10.8	4
5.	Medical facilities for your family.	14.8	32.5	32.2	11.3	9.2

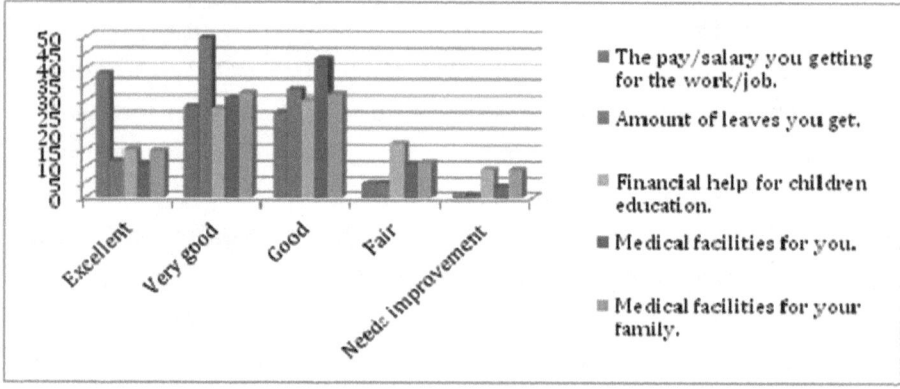

Figure 42: Employee engagement factors related to salary and other facilities (white collared employees)

When asked the white collared employees about pay and other facilities provided by organizations, 92% employees are happy with salary they get. 95% employees are happy with the leaves they get. 73% employees are satisfied with the financial help for child education while 85% employees are satisfied with medical facilities for them and 79% employees are happy with medical facilities for their family.

Training and development

Training & development is integral part of the employee engagement and job satisfaction. When employee knows about his job role, duties and responsibilities, qualification and skill matches to the given job. He uses his fullest potential to finish the job effectively. To update his knowledge and to furnish his skills, he needs to go under the training and development program. It not only will increase his efficiency but also helps him to lead in his career i.e. career advancement.

Most organisations link their goals with the training objectives unlike traditional system where in organisations used to believe and execute a stereo typed training sessions with out any objectives and even expectation of any desired results/benefits merely as other companies do we should also do it spirit.

As times have changed Training & Development has become a strategic intervention for improved performance in current scenario and during growth period.

Current day training & development system very clear draws training needs indicators (TNI) of employees and in term organisation every year. TNIs are drawn using following sources & process:

a. TNI forms: Voluntary inputs from Employees duly validated by the HODs as many cases employees express their nomination even for the course which would not need currently and also in future.

b. PMS: TNI recommended by HODs and reviewers are extracted for training calendar.

c. Interview process (Gaps from interview evaluations about the new joinee): As we never find 100% perfect candidates, during the interview process organisations draw the gaps and ensure the training imparted for desired performance.

f. Process Failures: TNI also drawn from the process failures revealed through Route Cause Analysis of customer complaints wherein if Human error has been identified which suggests refresher training to a particular employees.

g. Accidents/incidents: TNI also is drawn from incidents/accidents occurred, if Route Cause Analysis of the same reveals Human Error than necessary training need to be imparted.

h. Developmental plan: If any HOD is planning to an employee for promotion over 1–2 years he conveys TNI gaps for the new role to the HR manager for imparting training.

i. Succession plan: Organisations make 3–5 yrs Succession plan which also indicate various TNI for all the recommended employees, which is included in the Training calendars by the HR departments.

j. New Business model/additional business model: When an organisation in its process of growth &improvement plans for new business model or add a new business model TNI Gaps are filled by the HR department for organisational success.

k. Merger & Acquisition or Joint ventures: Organisation's during their process of growth do enter business deals termed as Merger & Acquisitions or at times Joint ventures which essentially come with huge challenge of Organisational change posing large gaps of skills, cultures, process, moral & ethics between the indulging organisations. HR managers along with strategic teams draw out training & development plan and meet the challenges.

Types of Training & Development Process

As training & development have become scientific and goal oriented for the organisational success and growth; hence, there are various types of trainings that meet the organisational needs such as:

Types of Training

a. Class room instructions: This is conducted in house using internal instructors who considered to be best persons to understand challenge and also impart the right content knowing learning capabilities of employees at individual level. Such trainers are most effective in meeting organisational goals. For some of the new skills acquisition external trainers are also hired who in a defined time frame transfer the knowledge effectively.

    Mostly, organisations feel that as far as behavioural training is concerned external trainers are more effective as they engage employees very quickly and make them comfortable involving in role playing type of exercises etc.

    Mostly technical/process trainings are best undertaken by in house trainers and are able to transfer/update skills and process to the employees in desired time frame.

b. On job/On site training: Every training unless improves application levels it remains a sermon which may or may not show effect when it comes to performance. Hence, after class room training On job practical training has very high impact on learnings through class room trainings in terms of transforming into application skills.

    There are few kinds of training which are more of action/activity base are imparted directly on site/on job for better and in quickest possible time period.

Conduct of Training & Learning Index

Prior & after to any training session a pre & post test is conduct which gives out the learning index of participant as to indicate how much learning has been attained by participant through the session.

Many companies maintain Learning index of employee which is used to understand learning capabilities of participants and also while selecting employees for a special course.

On completion of Training a feed back also is obtained from participants as to quality of training in terms of content, delivery and interaction level and about the trainer etc.

Training Impact & ROI

Once the either type of training is imparted by either of mode very important task is of mapping its impact which need to meet the bench mark of organisational goals through training for achieving organisational goals.

12 weeks post OJT (after class room training) HODs are tasked by the HR departments to fill up a report indicating pre training and post training improvements in performance of the employee.

There are professionally managed organisations which even go to the extent of calculating ROI from training as Training is cost head and has organisation's financial objectives, which are on developmental stage and more so there are many components of training cost which are either common facto or not relevant etc.

So the questions were asked related to training and development programs in the organization. It showed that nearly 76% blue collared employees and 64.5% white collared employees are happy and satisfied with the training given them in the induction period. Nearly 38.5% of white collared employees are completely happy with the tool and techniques used for training. Nearly 55% blue collared employees and 47.50% white collared employees felt connected to the trainer as well as the content of training program. Nearly 69% blue collared employees and 68% white collared employees would like to undergo T & D program for the betterment of their job and feel that this will help them to improve in their job and help them to go ahead in their career. The most of the organizations provide training on job i.e. 61% while in classroom 20% training is given and some of the organizations provide both types of training.

Blue collared employees

Table 30: Does the Organization provide training whenever necessary?(BCE)

Scale	No. of employees	Percentage
Yes	454	75.7
No	146	24.3
Total	600	100.0

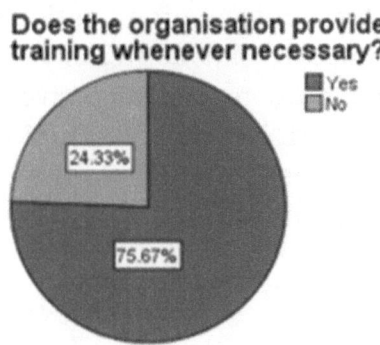

Figure 43: Does the Organization provide training whenever necessary?(BCE)

Training for blue coloured employee is very critical as they need to play their roles without error as their error cost organisations huge in terms of waste, re process cost etc. When the Question was posed to them, nearly 75% blue collared employees think that they get training whenever necessary.

Table 31: Are you satisfied with the training programme which has been given to you in past? (BCE)

Scale	No. of employees	Percentage
Totally	80	13.3
Almost	245	40.8
Sometimes	171	28.5
Never	104	17.3
Total	600	100.0

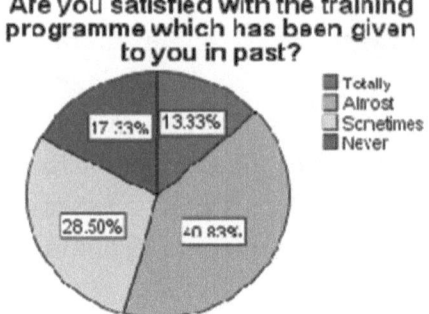

Figure 44: Are you satisfied with the training programme which has been given to you in past? (BCE)

To achieve organisational objectives it is very important to ensure that contents of training conduct are relevant and contribute to the objectives. When employees were aske the Question, Nearly 13% employees are totally satisfied while 41% are almost satisfied. So the care should be taken to improve the quality of training.

Table 32: Did you feel connected with your trainer and instructors during the course of the training programme ? (BCE)

Scale	No. of employees	Percentage
Completely	81	13.5
Yes, To an Extent	332	55.3
Sometimes	183	30.5
Not at all	4	.7
Total	600	100.0

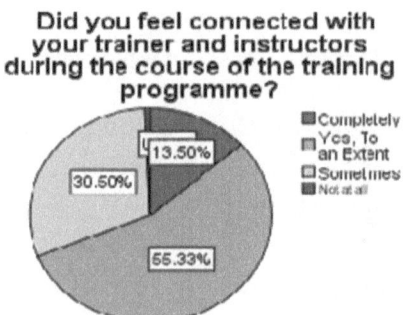

Figure 45: Did you feel connected with your trainer and instructors during the course of the training programme?(BCE

Nearly 14% employees think they were completely connected to trainer while 55% think they were connected to an extent to trainer.

Table 33: Would you like to undergo training and development to improve in your work? (BCE)

option	No. of employees	Percentage
Yes	414	69.0
No	186	31.0
Total	600	100.0

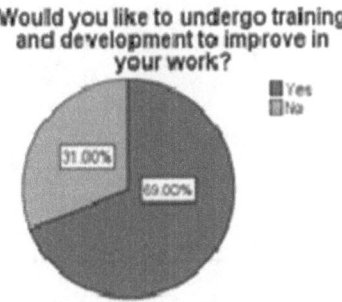

Figure 46: Would you like to undergo training and development to improve in your work? (BCE)

Nearly 69% employees would like to undergo training programs to improve their work.

Table 34: Do you think training program will help you to perform better on the job from now on? (BCE)

option	No. of employees	Percentage
Definitely	75	12.5
Yes	373	62.2
Maybe	149	24.8
Never	3	.5
Total	600	100.0

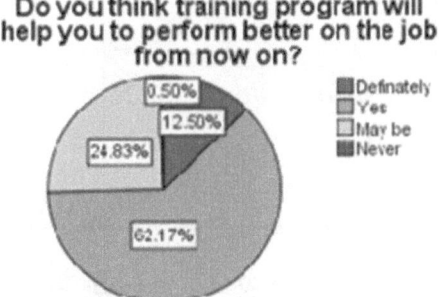

Figure 47: Do you think training program will help you to perform better on the job from now on? (BCE)

Nearly 12% employees think that it will help them to improve their work definitely while 62% also think positively about it.

Table 35: Does the Organization provides training whenever necessary?(BCE)

option	No. of employees	Percentage
Yes	454	75.7
No	146	24.3
Total	600	100.0

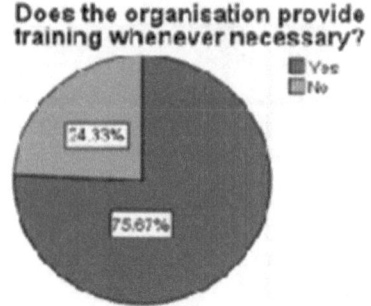

Figure 48: Does the Organization provides training whenever necessary?(BCE)

Nearly 75% employees think that organizations provide them training whenever necessary.

Table 36: Are you satisfied with the training programme which has been given to you in past? (BCE)

Option	No. of employees	Percentage
Totally	80	13.3
Almost	245	40.8
Sometimes	171	28.5
Never	104	17.3
Total	600	100.0

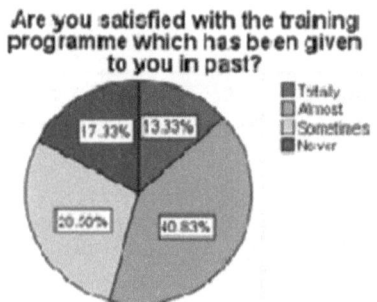

Figure 49: Are you satisfied with the training programme which has been given to you in past? (BCE)

Quality of Trainers

Training is activity which needs active involvement of both Trainer and participants as it cannot be imparted mechanically where Trainer just delivers the content. Unless trainer quickly builds up rapport with the participant the session will be monotonous and participants will not be able to concentrate, not be alert and will not be able to involve during the session, which will affect their learning from the training session. This is because the will not able to concentrate and involve and will not be able to raise the query which may help give complete learning from the training session.

To ensure theses HR managers when select the Trainers not only ensure that the content is relevant to the gap but also are lively in delivery of content making it interactive and interesting, this is ensured by mock session conducted in the presence of few executives of concerned department and support departments.

Table 37: Did you feel connected with your trainer and instructors during the course of the training programme? (BCE)

Option	No. of employees	Percentage
Completely	81	13.5
Yes, To an Extent	332	55.3
Sometimes	183	30.5
Not at all	4	.7
Total	600	100.0

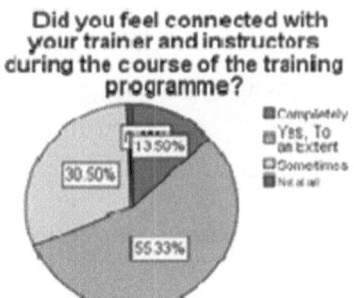

Figure 50: Did you feel connected with your trainer and instructors during the course of the training programme? (BCE

Nearly 13% employees feel completed connected to trainer while 55% feel connected to an extent. Which is good score since any training session is considered productive as long as it delivers satisfactorily for 60–70% of participants. As not all participants are all the time involved and alert during the session.

Table 38: Does the organization provide class room training or job training? (BCE)

Option	No. of employees	Percentage
Classroom	112	18.7
On job	366	61.0
Both	122	20.3
Total	600	100.0

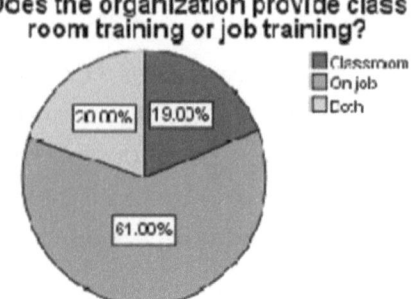

Figure 51: Does the organization provide class room training or job training? (BCE)

Table 39: Do you think that T & D given by the Organization help your career development/promotions and skill improvement?(BCE)

Option	No. of employees	Percentage
Yes	374	62.3
No	226	37.7
Total	600	100.0

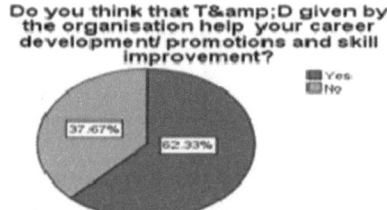

Figure 52: Do you think that T & D given by the Organization help your career development/promotions and skill improvement?(BCE)

62.3% employees relied in affirmative that Training and Development given by the organisations help their career development/promotions and skill development.

White collared employees

Table 40: Does the Organization provide training whenever necessary?(WCE)

Option	No. of employees	Percentage
Yes	385	64.2
No	215	35.8
Total	600	100.0

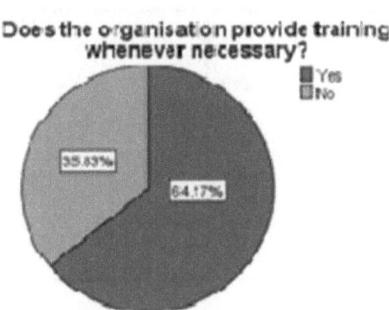

Figure 53: Does the Organization provide training whenever necessary?(WCE)

Nearly 64% employees feel that organization provide training whenever necessary.

Table 41: Are you satisfied with the training programme which has been given to you in past ? (WCE)

option	No. of employees	Percentage
Totally	168	28.0
Almost	111	18.5
Sometimes	190	31.7
Never	131	21.8
Total	600	100.0

Figure 54: Are you satisfied with the training programme which has been given to you in past? (WCE)

28%, 18% and 31% approx. employees has responded positive as Totally, Almost and sometimes satisfy with the training program.

Table 42: Are you satisfied with the techniques and tools used in the training programme ? (WCE)

Option	No. of employees	Percentage
Completely	230	38.3
Yes, To an Extent	90	15.0
Sometimes	213	35.5
Not at all	67	11.2
Total	600	100.0

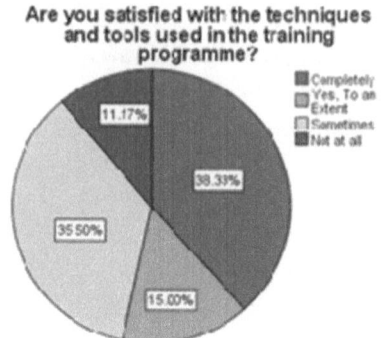

Figure 55: Are you satisfied with the techniques and tools used in the training programme ? (WCE)

Nearly 38% employees are satisfied completely while 15% are satisfied to an extent with the tools and techniques.

Table 43 Did you feel connected with your trainer and instructors during the course of the training programme ? (WCE)

option	No. of employees	Percentage
Completely	285	47.5
Yes, To an Extent	49	8.2
Sometimes	218	36.3
Not at all	48	8.0
Total	600	100.0

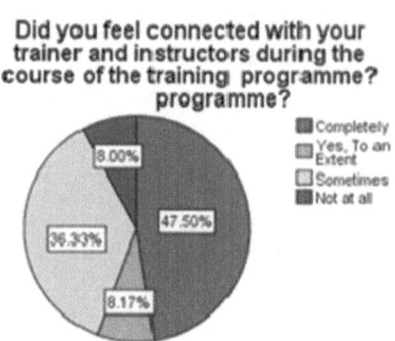

Figure 56: Did you feel connected with your trainer and instructors during the course of the training programme?(WCE)

Nearly 55% employees feel connected to trainer.

**Table 44: Would you like to undergo training and development
to improve in your work? (WCE)**

option	No. of employees	Percentage
Yes	406	67.7
No	194	32.3
Total	600	100.0

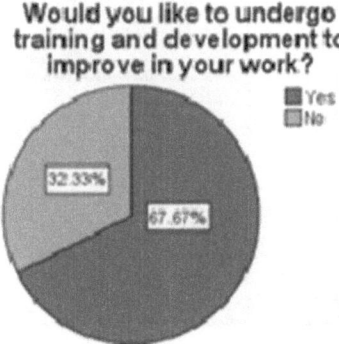

**Figure 57: Would you like to undergo training and development to improve in
your work? (WCE)**

Nearly 67% employees would like to undergo training to improve their work.

**Table 45: Do you think training program will help you to perform better on the
job from now on? (WCE)**

Option	No. of employees	Percentage
Definitely	225	37.5
Yes	97	16.2
Maybe	162	27.0
Never	116	19.3
Total	600	100.0

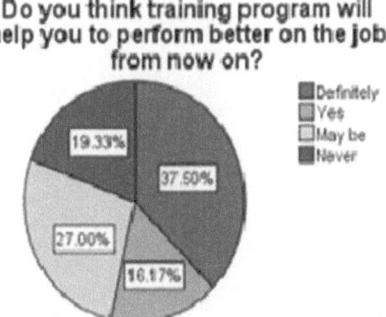

**Figure 58: Do you think training program will help you to perform better on the
job from now on? (WCE)**

Nearly 37% employees feel that training program is definitely going to help them perform better in job, while 16% feel it can help them perform better in the job.

153

Table 46: Do you think that T & D given by the Organization help your career development/promotions?

Option	No. of employees	Percentage
Yes	362	60.3
No	238	39.7
Total	600	100.0

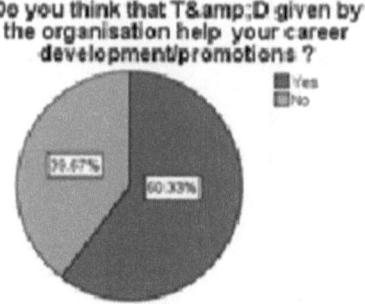

Figure 59: Do you think that T & D given by the Organization help your career development/promotion

Nearly 60% employees think that training given by organization will help them for career development and promotions.

Combined results

Table 47: Does the Organization provide training www? whenever necessary?

Option	Blue Collared Employees	White collared employees	Combined	Percentage
Yes	454	385	839	69.9916874
No	146	215	361	30.0083126
Total	600	600	1203	100

Figure 60: Does the Organization provide training whenever necessary?

Nearly 69% employees think that organization provides training whenever necessary.

Table 48: Are you satisfied with the training programme which has been given to you in past?

Option	Blue Collared Employees	White collared employees	Combined	Percentage
Totally	80	168	248	20.6666667
Almost	245	111	356	29.6666667
Sometimes	171	190	361	30.0833333
Never	104	131	235	19.5833333
Total	600	600	1200	100

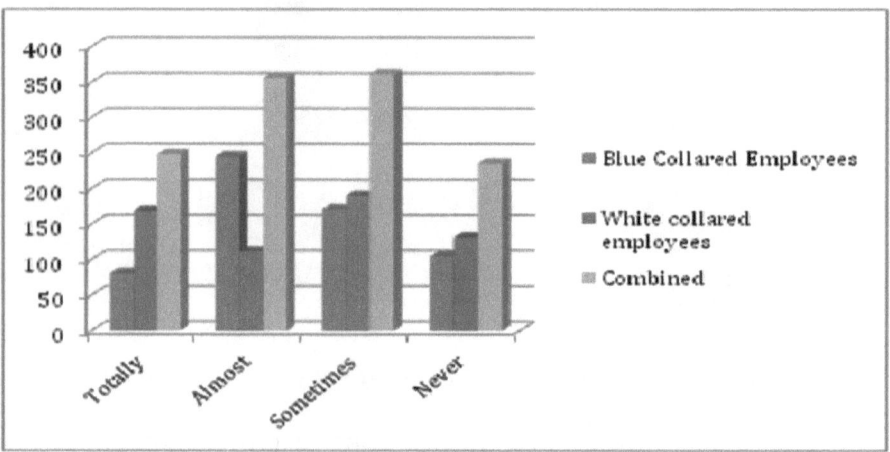

Figure 61: Are you satisfied with the training programme which has been given to you in past?

Nearly 20% employees feel totally while 29% feel almost satisfied with the training provided to them in the past.

Table 49: Did you feel connected with your trainer and instructors during the course of the training program?

Option	Blue Collared Employees	White collared employees	Combined	Percentage
Completely	81	230	311	25.9166667
Yes, To an Extent	332	90	422	35.1666667
Sometimes	183	213	396	33
Not at all	4	67	71	5.91666667
Total	600	600	1200	100

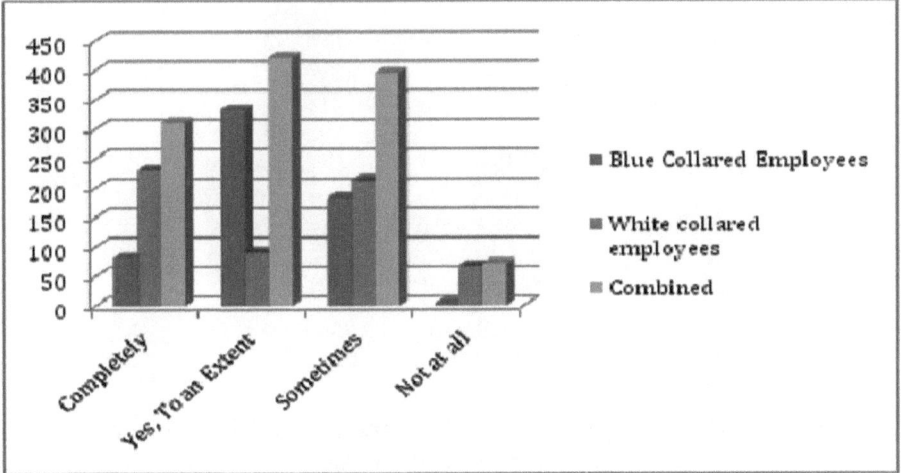

Figure 62: Did you feel connected with your trainer and instructors during the course of the training program?

Nearly 25% employee feel totally connected while 35% feel connected to trainer to an extent.

**Table 50: Would you like to undergo training and development
to improve in your work?**

Option	Blue Collared Employees	White collared employees	Combined	Percentage
Yes	414	406	820	68.3333333
No	186	194	380	31.6666667
Total	600	600	1200	100

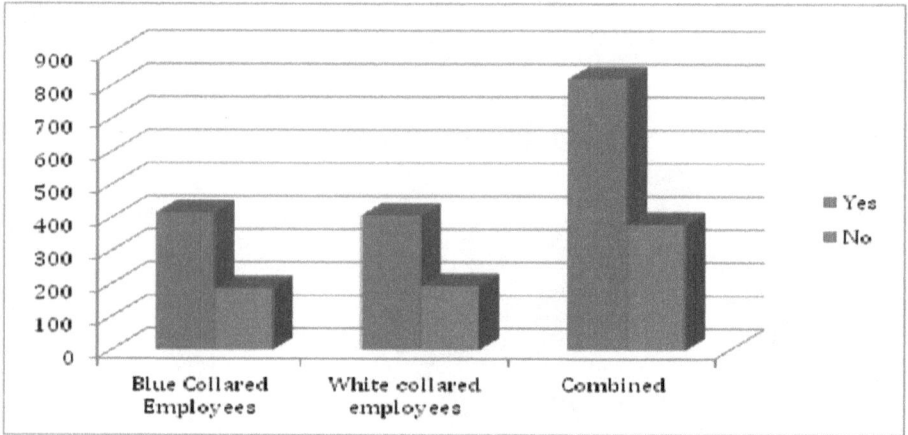

**Figure 63: Would you like to undergo training and development
to improve in your work?**

Nearly 68% would like to undergo training and development to improve their work. It shows that they are eager to engage in the given job.

Table 51: Do you think training program will help you to perform better on the job from now on?

Option	Blue Collared Employees	White collared employees	Combined	Percentage
Definitely	75	225	300	25
Yes	373	97	470	39.1666667
May be	149	162	311	25.9166667
Never	3	116	119	9.91666667
Total	600	600	1200	100

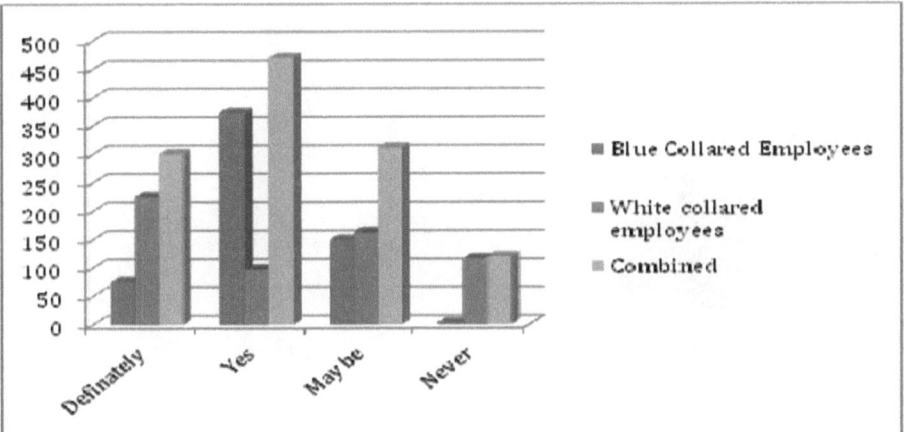

Figure 64: Do you think training program will help you to perform better on the job from now on?

Nearly 25% employees definitely think that training program will help you to perform better on the job from now on, and 39% employees think it can help them.

Table 52: Do you think that T & D given by the Organization help your career development/promotions?

Option	Blue Collared Employees	White collared employees	Combined	Percentage
Yes	374	362	736	61.3333333
No	226	238	464	38.6666667
Total	600	600	1200	100

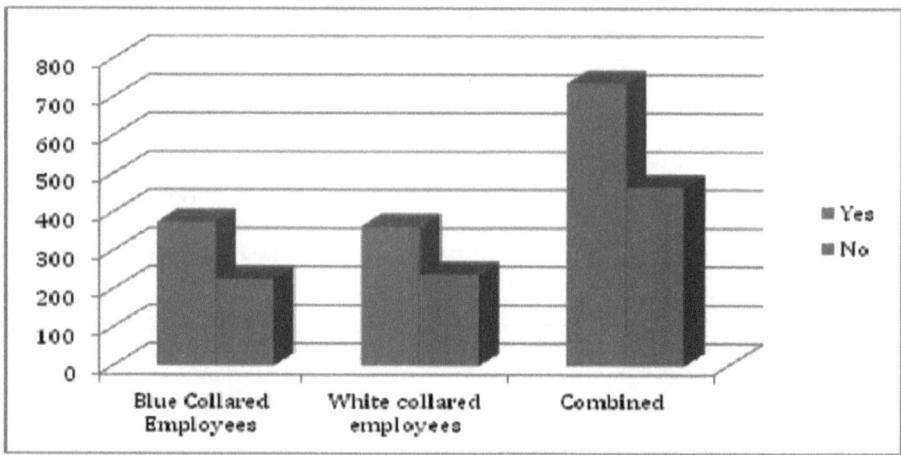

Figure 65: Do you think that T & D given by the Organization help your career development/promotions ?

Nearly 61% employees think that T & D given by the Organization help your career development/promotions.

Performance management

Dealing with performance is very crucial for employee engagement as almost all the category employees always expect their management to deal with the performance more pragmatically &fairly as it is for them is most crucial part of the employee engagement policy of the organization.

Days have been past when job roles were merely expected doing the job with out constituents of quality of out put & time line, but now in extremely competitive, customer ruled and socially & statutory complied market where margins shrinking every day definition of performance has changed to execution of task with expected quality and within time frame. Such situations pose huge pressure on the employees and organisations to meet the market need for survival and growth. These challenges forced the organisations and HR managers *per se* to evolve strategies to ensure that employees comply with the market need.

Over the time, employee performance management has become one of the major business critical objectives which can wait for things to turn around on its own with lapse of time.

As the business challenges are high on, and employees too have become very ambitious and their career & financial growth depends on performance and not on social relationship, a scientific Performance management system (PMS) becomes need of the organisation for satisfaction of employees and engagement & retention objectives of the organisation.

Of late following process of PMS which induces and enhances employee engagement in the organisations:

a. JD & KRA: This document lists out clearly the Job role of the employee with clarity on KRA, KPA and KPI with measurable parameter. These are defined through a open meeting between HOD and Reportee to reach agreement. In such meetings targets are discussed and also training (if needed) the administrative support provided to play the role as desired organisational goals.

b. Reference documents: During the discussion of KRAs it is also agreed as to which will be reference document to map the performance, these are auto generated MIS in case of SAP etc or where no MIS is generated to meet the objective such MIS is designed which is generated periodically by IT deptt to evaluate the performance.

c. Neutrality in performance management: As current days employees too have become aware about new trends of PMS, most organisations have implemented various systems i.e Balanced score card, 360 feed back, Bell Curve etc as per the professional generation of the organisation.

Compensation & Benefits

In olden times, employees used to be paid salaries and bonus etc as per statutory compliance and used to be good enough for their motivation and engagement, many of them used to work for whole life in same organisation and used to send their wards also.

With the change of times, many new initiatives have come in the HR processes as survival and growth of business is based on employees and customers. As competitions are becoming cut throat with decreasing margins organisations focused on addressing employee's issues:

a. Job satisfaction
b. Engagement
c. Well being
d. Retention
e. Pay & Allowances
f. Incentives
g. Perks & privileges

To address these issues the organisations have introduced following initiatives without even knowing its impacts except that these will give some positive impacts in engaging employees:

a. Retention bonus
d. Additional bonus
c. Personal accident cover
d. Medical coverage with family floater
e. Festival gifts
f. Paid family holidays

g. Flexi timing

h. 5 days week working

i. Overseas trips for tours & travel to best performing divisions/depart.

j. Variable pays

k. Performance based incentives (Unit, Division, SBU, Company performance)

l. Many others

Nearly 55% blue collared employees are not satisfied with the current appraisal process of their organization and they want to get it changed. Some have given suggestion to change in the increment system and basic salary structure. Nearly 67.5% employees are satisfied with promotional policies of the organization.

While for the white collared employees some extra questions were asked. Nearly 84.67% white collared employees get JD and KRAs defined for the year. Nearly 88.83 white collared employees think that PMS cover the key areas that focus on their personal growth. The recognition is based 57% seniority level and 39.50% on performance level. 72% white collared employees are happy with the promotional policies of the organization and 78.33% employees are happy with reward and recognition policies.

Blue collared employees

Table 53: Are you satisfied with the current appraisal process?(BCE)

Option	No. of employees	Percentage
Yes, very much satisfied	242	40.3
Not at all satisfactory	335	55.8
Needs an immediate amendment	15	2.5
The process is fine	8	1.3
Total	600	100.0

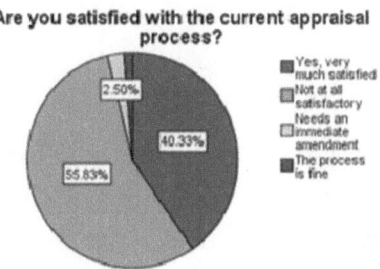

Figure 66: Are you satisfied with the current appraisal process?(BCE)

163

Only 37% employees are happy with the current appraisal process which is issue of concern.

Table 54: Are you happy with the promotional policies of organization? (BCE)

option	No. of employees	Percentage
Yes	405	67.5
No	195	32.5
Total	600	100.0

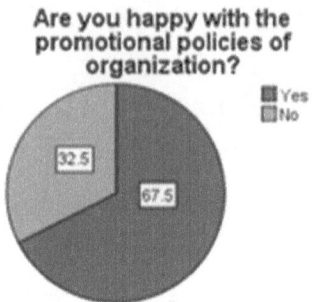

Figure 67: Are you happy with the promotional policies of organization? (BCE)

Nearly 67% employees are happy with the promotional policies of organization.

White collared employees

Table 55: Does the organization define your JD & KRAs? (WCE)

Option	No. of employees	Percentage
Yes	508	84.7
No	92	15.3
Total	600	100.0

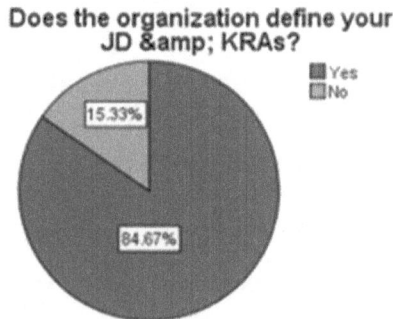

Figure 68: Does the organization define your JD & KRAs? (WCE)

Nearly 84% white collared employees think that organisation define their JD and KRAs properly. So they are aware about their duties and responsibilities

Table 56: According to you, does the performance management system cover the key areas that focus on your personal development? (WCE)

Option	No. of employees	Percentage
Yes	533	88.8
no,not at all	52	8.7
to some ex tent	15	2.5
Total	600	100.0

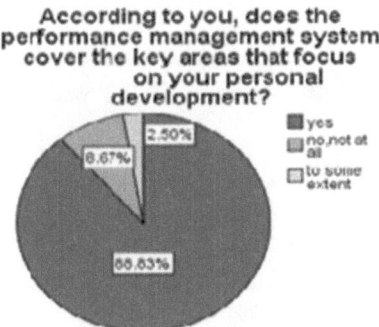

Figure 69: According to you, does the performance management system cover the key areas that focus on your personal development? (WCE)

Nearly 89% employees think that PMS cover the key areas that focus on their personal development.

Table 57: Do you think the recognitions are based on the performance or it has any other factor? (WCE)

Option	No. of employee	Percentage
they are based on performance	237	39.5
seniority based	342	57.0
not streamlined	21	3.5
Total	600	100.0

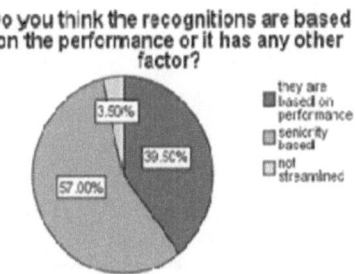

Figure 70: Do you think the recognitions are based on the performance or it has any other factor? (WCE)

Nearly 39% employees think that recognitions are based on performance, while 57% employees think that it is based on seniority.

Table 58: Are you happy with the promotional policies of organization?(WCE)

option	No. of employees	Percentage
Yes	432	72.0
No	168	28.0
Total	600	100.0

Are you happy with the promotional policies of organization?
■ Yes
☐ No
28.00%
72.00%

Figure 71: Are you happy with the promotional policies of organization? (WCE)

Nearly 72% white collared employees are happy with the promotional policies of the organization.

Table 59: Are you happy with rewards and recognitions policies of the organization?(WCE)

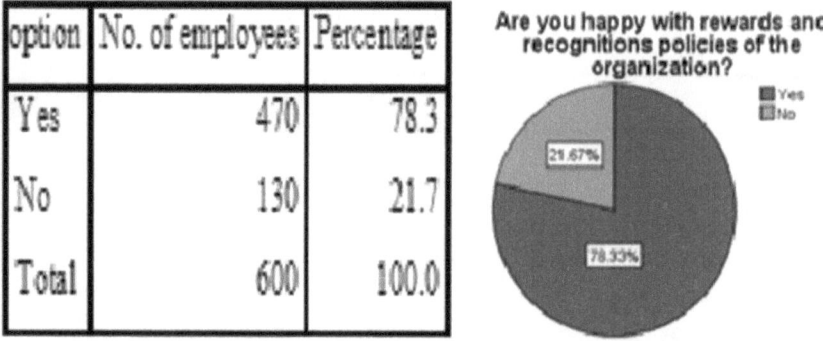

option	No. of employees	Percentage
Yes	470	78.3
No	130	21.7
Total	600	100.0

Are you happy with rewards and recognitions policies of the organization?
■ Yes
☐ No
21.67%
78.33%

Figure 72: Are you happy with rewards and recognitions policies of the organization? (WCE)

Nearly 78% white collared employees are happy with the reward and recognition policies.

Combined Results

Table 60: Are you satisfied with the current appraisal process?

Option	Blue Collared Employees	White collared employees	Combined	Percentage
Yes, very much satisfied	242	210	452	37.6666667
Not at all satisfactory	335	46	381	31.75
Needs an immediate amendment	15	305	320	26.6666667
The process is fine	8	39	47	3.91666667
Total	600	600	1200	100

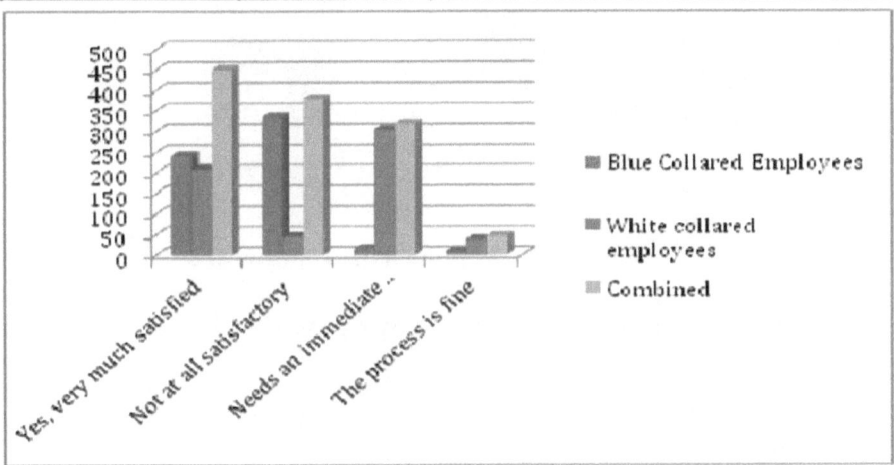

Figure 73: Are you satisfied with the current appraisal process?

Nearly 37% employees are satisfied with the current performance appraisal process.

Table 61: Are you happy with the promotional policies of organization?

Option	Blue Collared Employees	White collared employees	Combined	Percentage
Yes	405	432	837	69.75
No	195	168	363	30.25
Total	600	600	1200	100

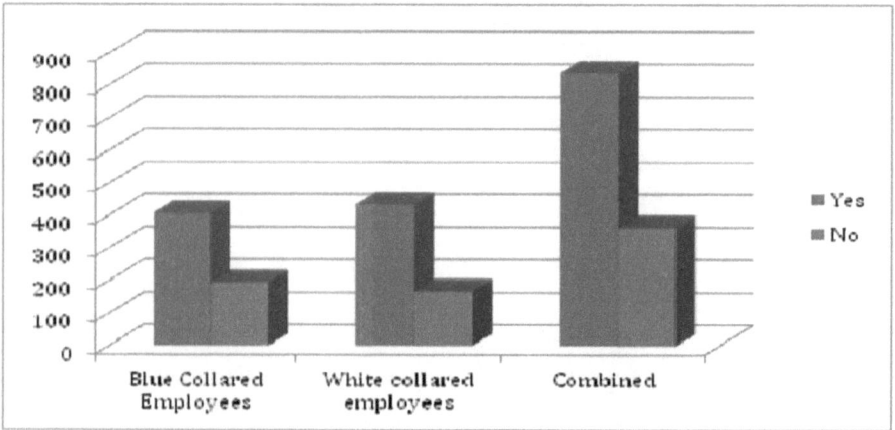

Figure 74: Are you happy with the promotional policies of organization?

Nearly 70% employees are happy with the promotional policies of the organization.

Miscellaneous

Ultimately one of the key goal organisations in today's business scenario strive for is engaged performing employee who bear loyalty to the organisation.

As not all employees who continue for long with organisation are not necessarily engaged similarly all long serving employee may not be loyal as well.

Qualities of Loyal Employees

a. They exhibit loyalty through Integrity

b. They Motivate peers to grow

c. They convey even to bosses on the decisions they don't agree but privately

d. They Dissent & dis agree on any issue where they have difference of opinion

e. They treat you like a person not like boss and accept your weakness equally as strength

f. They are Starter/Interactive in discussion on the issue Organisation growth/concerns

g. They Openly support management decisions

h. They will tell you when there is over in the organisation

Drivers of Employee Loyalty

Like employee engagement there few most partied drivers which induce and enhance Employee's loyalty as under:

1. Fair ness in role distribution, performance evaluation

2. Employer's Concern for work place environment, HR Policies, Management style

3. Rationalised pay & allowances

4. Feeling of fully occupied at work place, and Appreciation for employee's feedback & suggestions

5. Career growth opportunities

6. Significance of job role of employees

7. Work-life balance

8. Reputations of employers as Corporate brand

9. Response to employee reference programs to recommend known candidate

10. Autonomy, flexibility in working and role in decision making

Many researchers have suggested that organisations may be able to hire best talent of the market but retaining an engaged &

loyal talent is big challenge for the organisation. If an organisation is unable to build pool of such loyal employees when the chips in business cycle are down organisation will be left with only those not desired lot.

Therefore, many employers prefer to maintain mixture of employees i.e those who are not so competent but loyal and also those most competent but unestablished loyalty at all the times and continue to work on the most competent but unestablished loyalty class of employees.

Ways to induce/enhance employee loyalty

In order to develop performing, engaged and loyal pool of employees most organisations insist upon feed-back and analysis of following tools:

a. Employee satisfaction surveys
b. Work place environment surveys
c. Job Satisfaction surveys
d. Employee engagement surveys
e. Truthful employee exit interviews
f. Work-life balance survey

Inputs of these Surveys are analysed in detailed and inputs received are discussed put up to management with mitigation plan for approval for implementation.

Implementation of mitigation plan by HR department in the form of HR policy is executed across the group and monitored for its impacts and results periodically.

During this research questions were asked form all levels of employee to know how they are aligned with the organization goal and would they like to work for more years in the organization. The question basically tests the loyalty and their willingness to work in the organization and how they feel about the organization. Nearly half of the blue collared employees would like work with same organization for more than 2 years. While for white collared employees the mean years for future working are 1 to 2 years. Nearly 57% of blue collared employees and 52.3% white collared employees would like to recommend their friends or relatives the respective organization for work. 65.5% blue collared employees and 54% white collared employees would like to work extra to achieve the goal of the organization.

One crucial question was asked whether they would like to offer some suggestion to change the employee engagement policies, nearly 96% both blue collared and white collared employees refused to offer any suggestion. It depicted that they are happy with the most of the HR policies of the organization but some of the things should be taken care of by the organizations which are, the open door policy for the communication, transparency and visibility at all the levels of the management. The work culture and work environment plays a very important role in employee engagement apart from the salary, rewards and recognition. So the organizations should make their HR policies for the well-being of employees which will ultimately result in engagement and which will increase the organization performance.

Blue collared employee

Table 62: Would you like to work for next – years in the same Organization?(BCE)

option	No. of employees	Percentage
1 yr	136	22.7
2 yrs	266	44.3
3 yrs	171	28.5
4 yrs	17	2.8
More than 4 yrs	9	1.5
Total	600	100.0

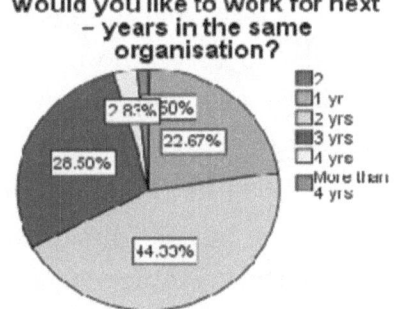

Figure 75: Would you like to work for next – years in the same Organization?(BCE)

Nearly 22% employees would like to work for 1 year, 44% for 2 years and 28% for 3 years. This shows their loyalty to the organization

Table 63: Would you recommend your friend/relative to work with this Organization? (BCE)

option	No. of employees	Percentage
Yes	343	57.2
No	257	42.8
Total	600	100.0

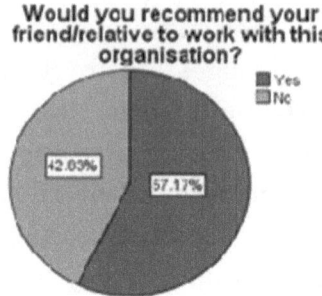

Figure 76: Would you recommend your friend/relative to work with this Organization? (BCE)

Employee Loyalty is premium that every management expect from the employee as they have been kept happy, satisfied and motivated all the time as due care has been taken of them and also family members in terms of Jobs satisfaction, career development, training & development etc for them while various facilities such as family medical policies, help in children educations, loan facility for housing and furniture etc.

All these personalised care taken by management it develops loyalty among employees which motivates employees not only work long term for organisation but also refer good candidates among their friend circle, relatives recommending the organisation as good employer to work with.

Most organisations who are sure that they are taking good care of their employees and their family members which has ensured most employees to be loyal to the organisation introduce many schemes such as employee referral schemes etc which allow them to refer their relatives/friends etc to apply for vacant positions with their organisation.

Such initiatives not only gives new pool of possible loyal employees but also help reducing recruitment costs and time taken for team building etc, hence some

Organisations have also started giving a notional amount to employee who refer a candidate who successfully qualify the selection process. This further motivates employees to refer candidates to the organisation.

Nearly 57% employees would like to recommend their friends and relatives the organization

Table 64: Would you like to give extra efforts to achieve the goal of the Organization?(BCE)

option	No. of employees	Percentage
Yes	391	65.2
No	209	34.8
Total	600	100.0

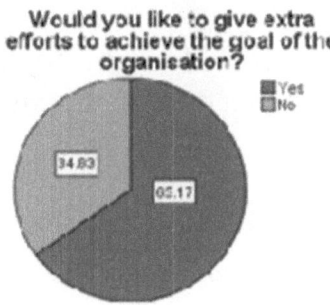

Figure 77: Would you like to give extra efforts to achieve the goal of the Organization?(BCE)

Nearly 65% employees would like to give extra efforts for the organization. This shows their loyalty to the organization.

Table 65: Would you like to offer suggestion to improve employee satisfaction levels?(WCE)

option	No. of employees	Percentage
Yes	20	3.33
No	578	96.67
Total	600	100.0

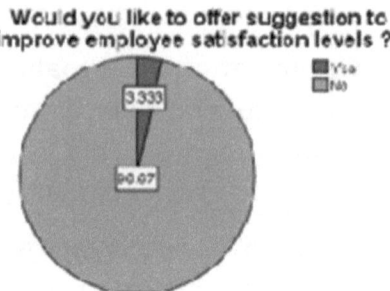

Figure 78: Would you like to offer suggestion to improve employee satisfaction levels ? (WCE)

Nearly 3% employees would like to suggest improving satisfaction level in organization which shows that employees are satisfied in the organization.

Table 66: Would you like to work for next – years in the same Organization?

Option	Blue Collared Employees	White collared employees	Combined	Percentage
1 yr	136	120	256	21.3333333
2 yrs	266	197	463	38.5833333
3 yrs	172	156	328	27.3333333
4 yrs	17	105	122	10.1666667
More than 4 yrs	9	22	31	2.58333333
Total	600	600	1200	100

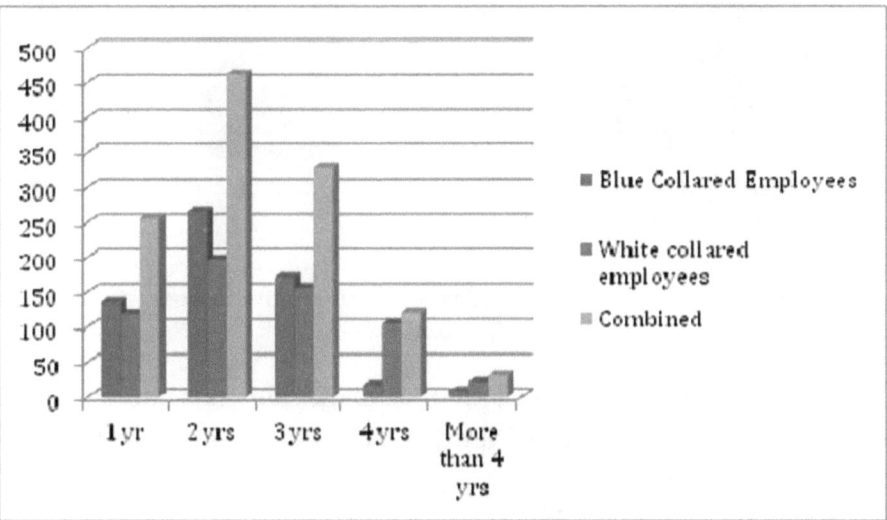

Figure 79: Would you like to work for next – years in the same Organization?

21% 38% and 27% responded that they would like to continue with their organisation for 1, 2 & 3 years respectively.

Table 67: Would you recommend your friend/relative to work with this Organization?

Option	Blue Collared Employees	White collared employees	Combined	Percentage
Yes	343	315	658	54.8333333
No	257	285	542	45.1666667
Total	600	600	1200	100

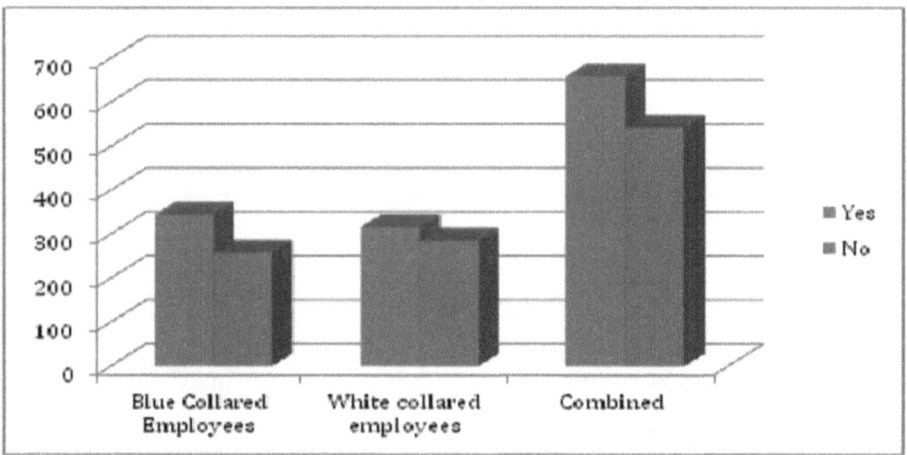

Figure 80: Would you recommend your friend/relative to work with this Organization?

55% employees responded in affirmative as that they will certainly recommend their friends/relatives to apply for vacancy in the organisation.

Table 68: Would you like to give extra efforts to achieve the goal of the Organization?

Option	Blue Collared Employees	White collared employees	Combined	Percentage
Yes	391	324	715	59.5833333
No	209	276	485	40.4166667
Total	600	600	1200	100

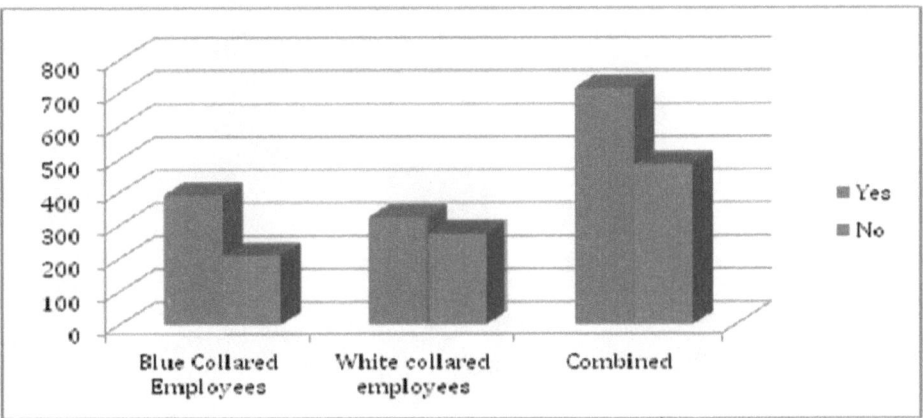

Figure 81: Would you like to give extra efforts to achieve the goal of the Organization?

59% employees responded that they are willing to give extra efforts to achieve the goal of the organisation.

Table 69: Would you like to offer suggestion to improve employee satisfaction levels ?

Option	Blue Collared Employees	White collared employees	Combined	Percentage
Yes	22	23	45	3.75
No	578	577	1155	96.25
Total	600	600	1200	100

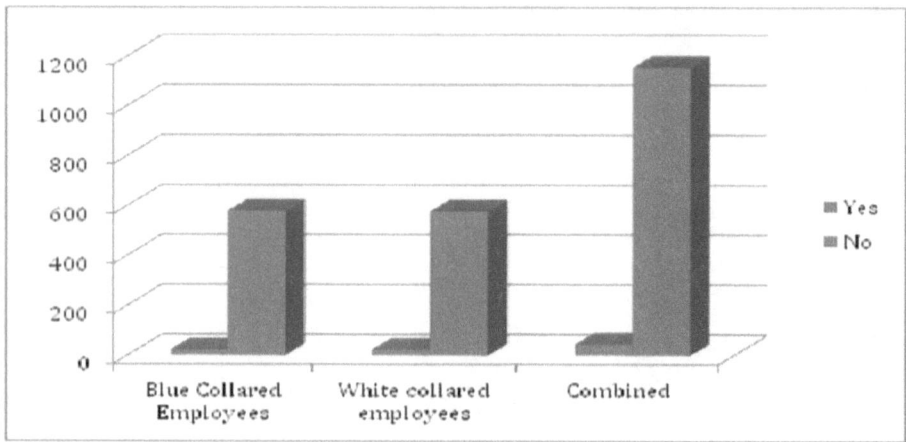

Figure 82: Would you like to offer suggestion to improve employee satisfaction levels ?

Only 3% employees responded that they would like to give suggestions to improve employee satisfaction as they feel that most of the employees are engaged.

HR Managers

India Inc has come a long way in accepting a global reality that HR function is key business function for any organisation to perform, sustain, grow and establish globally.

Like other business functions HR functions i.e Manpower planning, Recruitment & Talent management, Training & Development, Compensation & Benefit, Performance management, Rewards & recognition, employee motivation retention, employee welfare, employee engagement, Industrial relations, Statutory compliance need strategic planning with cost implications considerations.

The role of HR managers is not restricted to make plans but also align them with business plan of the organisation with goals & time lines and execute successfully. Even after implementation more important is to sustain and continuous improvement through inputs received from various employee survey.

Sometimes employee surveys inputs are so harsh that it shakes the HR manager's confidence as it similar to challenging his suitability to the assignment, in such situations HR managers have to recast the whole strategy and process.

Keeping in above view HR managers were included in the research for seeking response as they are the one who can give first hand input on the effective ness of various employee engagement policies implemented across industries surveyed.

The HR managers were also interviewed for the survey to know the HR policies of the organization and effectively they are working for the employees of the organization. They are asked about the different employee engagement policies about the organization, the overall work culture of the organization, work environment and the salary, Rewards and recognition policies as well as annual meetings, and get together for employees family. The study was done to see the compatibility of questionnaire related to HR policies of the organization.

Table 70: Statistics

Parameters	What is your turn over rate this fiscal year?	What is the attrition rate for last five years?	What percentage of management positions at the following levels has succession plans in place?	Please state the percentage of employees recruited through lateral entry.	Please state the percentage of employees recruited through internal promotions/shifting.
Mean	7.2320	6.92	48.6800	80.66	19.34
Median	5.0000	6.88	50.0000	80.00	20.00
Mode	5.00	10	80.00	80	20
Std. Deviation	9.22000	3.186	30.27051	13.868	13.868
Variance	85.008	10.148	916.304	192.311	192.311
Range	49.00	13	85.00	88	88

This statistical table shows the various measures taken to study about the attrition rate. The mean turnover rate of the year is 7.23 while median and mode are 5. Std. Deviation is 9.22. Likewise the mean for last five years turnover rate is 6.92 with median 6.88 and mode 10 with std. Deviation 3.186. The Attrition rates of the organisation surveyed were found well within bench mark for the Manufacturing Industry which is around 14% in year 2013.

One more question was asked about the succession plan of the organization. For which positions the succession plan is done and what are the percentages of management levels are at place. As shown in the above table the mean percentage is 48.68% while median is 50% and mode is 80% with std. Deviation 30.27%.

After the succession plan in place, one more important question was asked about the recruitment for vacated or new positions, whether it is done through lateral entry or internal up gradation. The responses were, mean 80.66% was through lateral entry with median 80%, mode 80% and std. Deviation 13.86%. Similarly the internal promotions/hiring responses were, mean 19.34%, median 20%, mode 20% with std. Deviation 13.86.

The other question asked to HR managers about the HR policies of Organisation, Training programs, Performance management system, other facilities, compensation and employee branding which are directly related to employee engagement and so the employee wellbeing, employee & organisational performance.

Manpower planning

Manpower planning is one of the task which every HR manager insists upon the management so that they can strategically hire the employees and also keep the manpower cost under budgeted.

To achieve the organisations have system of Annual Business Plan presentation by various Business heads wherein they not only forecast their top and bottom line as per management growth plan for the ensuing financial year.

This plan also give projection about additional/replacement manpower to meet the organisational goals.

Table 71: Does the Organisation has manpower plan?

Option	No. of employees	Percentage
Yes	43	86.0
No	7	14.0
Total	50	100.0

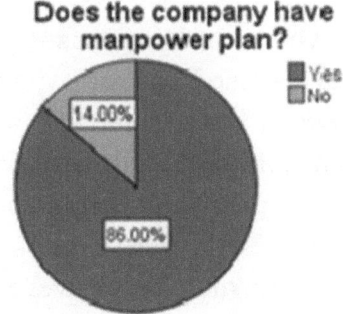

Does the company have manpower plan?

Figure 83: Does the Organisation has manpower plan?

181

When HR Managers were asked "Does the Organisation has manpower plan ?" 86% HR managers responded that their organisations have manpower plan.

Competency Mapping

Competency is defined as set of essentials traits that are considered must for an employee to perform his job role. Competency is mix of domain knowledge and behavioural traits which enable an employee perform successfully at job role to meet target.

Competency mapping is a process which measures an employee's inherent and acquired knowledge, skill and behavioural pattern using various methodologies.

Process for developing Competency mapping

a. Conduct Job Analysis through a questionnaire termed as PIQ (position information questionnaire) seeking info from employees as to what they feel the skills, behavioural pattern etc needed for the role.

b. Based on Job analysis, competency based Job description is designed and the same is used for performance evaluation of respective employee.

c. The inputs of competency mapping in terms of Technical & behavioural skills will needed for the role can also be used TNA for Training plan.

Once and organisation has competency based JDs, same can be used for interviewing the candidates to make interview process more scientific and help selecting right person for the right job with right attitude. As we donot get candidate 100% fit for the positions, while conducting in interview once a candidate is finalised, minor gaps needed in competencies for the job role can also be conveyed to the HR department for planning candidate's training session at the time of induction or as indicated by the HOD.

Methodology for Competency Mapping

Identifying competencies of all the positions through traditional methodology is a difficult task, hence there are number of methodologies in practices across the globe which have been able to meet challenge of managers and use it for identifying and, applying these for individual and organisational growth through recruiting, developing employees most fit for the job roles resulting into optimized performance of employee towards employee and organisational growth.

Most used Methodology for conducting Competency mapping are as under:

a. **Assessment Centre: This follows series of activities to generate competency report**

   i)   Interview simulations/Role Plays

   ii) Group Discussion

   iii) In tray (Situation appreciation through reading through old correspondence)

   iv) Case studies/Analysis Exercise

b. **Critical Incidents Techniques**

   i)   Unstructured approach

   ii) Moderate approach

c. **Interview Techniques Competency Mapping**

d. **Questionnaires**

   i)   Multipurpose Occupational System Analysis Inventory (MOSAIC)

   ii) Functional Job Analysis

   iii) Common Metric Questionnaire (CMQ)

   iv) Occupational Analysis Inventory

   v)   Work Profiling System (WPS)

   vi) Position Analysis Questionnaire (PAQ)

e. **Psychometric Testing**

    i)   Achievement Tests

    ii)   Aptitude Test

Table 72: Does every position have competency mapped for role ?

Option	No. of employees	Percentage
Yes	36	72.0
No	14	28.0
Total	50	100.0

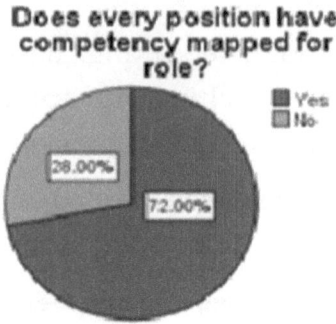

Figure 84: Does every position have competency mapped for role?

When question was asked from HR managers "Does every position have competency mapped for role ?" 72% HR managers responded that their organisations, have conducted competency for every position.

Table 73: Does every employee understand Competency/requirement needed to perform a job/position?

Option	No. of employees	Percentage
Yes	45	90.0
No	5	10.0
Total	50	100.0

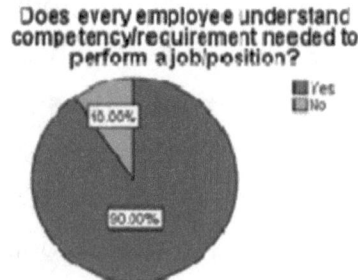

Figure 85: Does every employee understand Competency/requirement needed to perform a job/position?

Findings: 86% HR mangers say that they have manpower planning. 72% of HR managers agree that every position have competency mapped for role. And 66% say that every employee understands competency/requirement needed to perform a job/position. It infers that all the position has employees with matching skills, so that it not only help them in employee engagement but also helps them use their full potential.

Retention

Till 1970s, India had Industries which were set up during British rule owned by Tatas, Birlas, Thapers etc, hence Employees did not have much choice than to join one of the Factory owned by these groups only, hence organisation never faced attrition as challenge. Further, the skill sets need were very commonly available and there was not Training conducted in the organisations except safety related training.

As decade of 1980–90 turned, India witness globalisation wherein many MNCs started entering Indian markets putting up plants bringing new age Technology machinery followed by entry Automation in the most critical processing plants. This industrial revolution not only brought many job opportunities posing "Retention as New Challenge" for organisations but also "Skill based challenges" for employees to continue/change for new job opportunity as by this time employee were expected to have/obtain higher & newer skill sets for current job and also for job change.

To undertake these challenge, organisations introduced extensive skill development programs to upgrade/sharpen skill sets of existing employee and simultaneously ambitious employees too started acquiring new skills at their own cost for their own market value.

Above initiative gave immediate impacts to the organisation which was followed by introduction of luring tricks to tap efficient employees of competitors, which triggered cut throat competitions resulting into welfare measures, work place environments, employee canteen facilities, family hospitals, better schools, motivational activities to engage families e.g celebration of Dushera, Diwali festivals, Religious plays, Kavi sammelan, mushaira etc to introduce **"feel good factor"** among employees.

These initiative contained the attrition to great extent and thereafter extensive training was introduce to retain the employee, few select employees used to be sent abroad for seminars/ conferences/course etc which triggered "Retention" further.

Table 74: Do you track your staff turnover?

Option	No. of employees	Percentage
Yes	47	94.0
No	3	6.0
Total	50	100.0

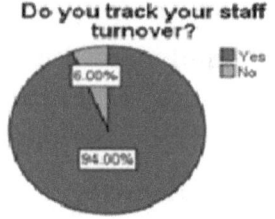

Figure 86: Do you track your staff turnover?

When HR manager's were asked Question "Do you track turnover ?" 94% HR managers responded in affirmation which indicates that most organisation take retention as major challenge and put in continuous & innovative efforts in meeting retention targets considering critical organisational goal.

Table 75: Does the Organisation develop attractive benefit program that can retain employees?

option	No. of employees	Percentage
Yes	33	66.0
No	17	34.0
Total	50	100.0

Figure 87: Does the Organisation develop attractive benefit program that can retain employees?

When HR managers were asked "Does the Organisation develop attractive benefit program that can retain employees ?" 66% HR managers responded in affirmation. This points that organisation's make serious efforts to develop "employee benefit programs"

Table 76: Do the current HR policies and employee engagement policies help in employee retention?

option	No. of employees	Percentage
Yes	46	92.0
No	4	8.0
Total	50	100.0

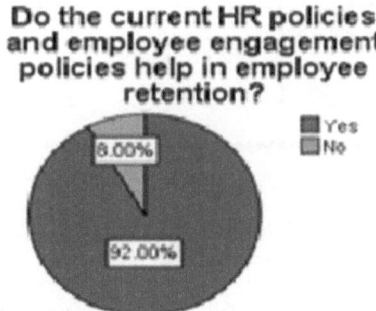

Figure 88: Do the current HR policies and employee engagement policies help in employee retention

When asked about staff turnover record, nearly 94% HR managers told that their organization track the record. While 66% employees say that they develop attractive benefit program that can retain employees like salary hike, good welfare activities, working environment, suggestion box, Gratuity, superannuation, group mediclaim, compensation and benefits - short term and long term, retention bonus, talent mapping, stock options only for GM level. So nearly 92% of the organization's HR policies help in employee retention.

Training and development of employee

Table 77: Does the Organisation have a clear development or training plan/strategy?

Option	No. of employees	Percentage
Yes	43	86.0
No	7	14.0
Total	50	100.0

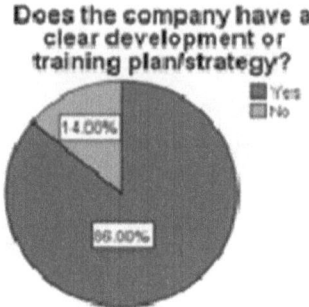

Figure 79: Does the Organisation have a clear development or training plan/strategy

Nearly 86% of the organisations have clear training plan for the employees.

Table 78: Does the organization asks feedback to employees about training and development programme?

Option	No. of employees	Percentage
Yes	40	80.0
No	10	20.0
Total	50	100.0

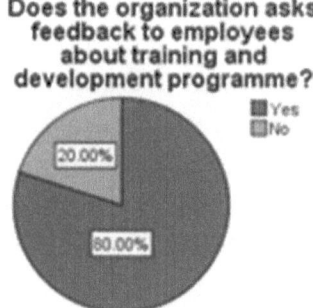

Figure 90: Does the organization asks feedback to employees about training and development programme?

Nearly 80% of the organisations ask feedback about the training and development programme.

Table 79: Are the employees benefited by training and development programs conducted by organization?

Option	No. of employees	Percentage
Yes	50	100.0

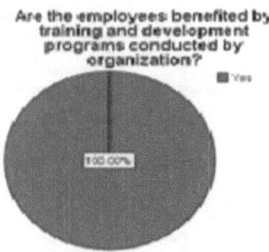

Figure 91: Are the employees benefited by training and development programs conducted by organization?

All the organisations think that employees are benefited by training and development programmes.

When asked about training and development system of the organization, 86% organizations have a clear development or training plan/strategy. And 80% of the organizations ask feedback to employees about training and development program.

All the organizations unanimously agree that the employees are benefited by training and development programs conducted by organization. Training and development is important part of engagement as it leads to better job performance, better career and so better well-being and satisfied employee.

Performance management

Table 80: Do you give constructive feedback to increase employee's performance?

Option	No. of employees	Percentage
Yes	37	74.0
No	13	26.0
Total	50	100.0

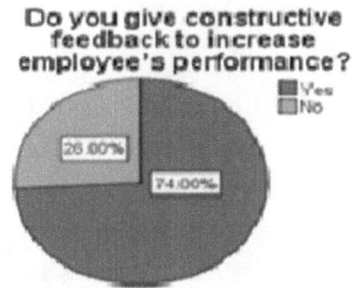

Figure 92: Do you give constructive feedback to increase employee's performance?

Table 81: Do you include a customer satisfaction element in performance evaluations?

Option	No. of employees	Percentage
Yes	23	46.0
No	27	54.0
Total	50	100.0

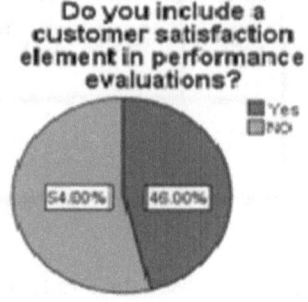

Figure 93: Do you include a customer satisfaction element in performance evaluations?

Only 46% of the organisations include customer satisfaction element in performance management.

Table 82: Do you carry the feedback survey for employees to measure the impact of HR policies and employee engagement programs on their performance?

Option	No. of employees	Percentage
Yes	20	40.0
No	30	60.0
Total	50	100.0

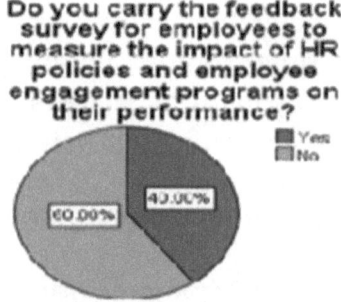

Figure 94: Do you carry the feedback survey for employees to measure the impact of HR policies and employee engagement programs on their performance?

When asked about the current performance management system, various systems are used. Most commonly used are Bell curve, 360 degree feedback, PMS and MBO systems. 74% HR Managers said that their organisation's do seek employee's inputs to monitor as to how HR policies are constructively help improve employee's productivity. 46% organizations include customer satisfaction as one of the criteria for performance appraisal which 54% organizations do not agree with it. Nearly 40% organizations carry the feedback survey for employees to measure the impact of HR policies and employee engagement programs on their performance. It is important to get feedback from employees as it will help planning or modifying HR policies accordingly.

Career development and succession planning

Table 83: Do succession plan exist for all critical positions?

Option	No. of employees	Percentage
Yes	28	56.0
No	22	44.0
Total	50	100.0

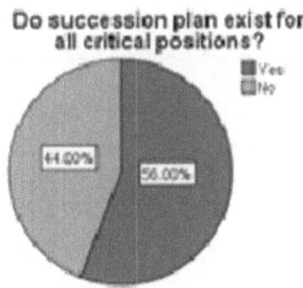

Figure 95: Do succession plan exist for all critical positions?

Employee communication

Table 84: Do you have an environment of open communication between employees and management?

Option	No. of employees	Percentage
Yes	42	84.0
No	8	16.0
Total	50	100.0

Figure 96: Do you have an environment of open communication between employees and management?

Nearly 89% organisations have open communication environment.

Table 85: Do you capture the creative insight of employees by soliciting their ideas for improvement?

Option	No. of employees	Percentage
Yes	46	92.0
No	4	8.0
Total	50	100.0

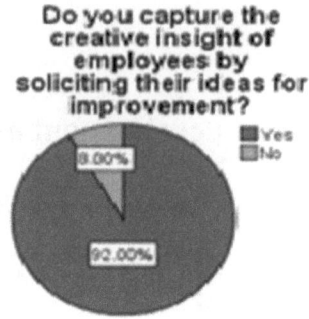

Figure 97: Do you capture the creative insight of employees by soliciting their ideas for improvement?

Nearly 92% organisations have vision for the creativity of employees and they solicit their ideas.

Table 86: Do you provide any platform to present their ideas?

Option	No. of employees	Percentage
Yes	42	84.0
No	8	16.0
Total	50	100.0

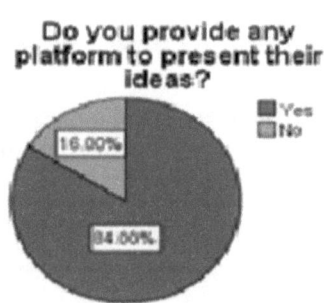

Figure 98: Do you provide any platform to present their ideas?

Nearly 84% organisations provide employees a platform to present their ideas.

Table 87: Do you circulate the ideas in weekly meeting?

Option	No. of employees	Percentage
Yes	23	46.0
No	27	54.0
Total	50	100.0

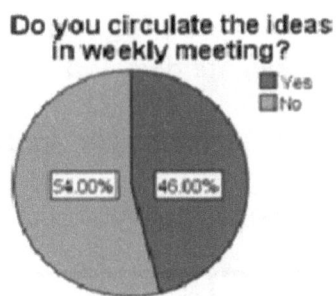

Figure 99: Do you circulate the ideas in weekly meeting?

Only 46% organisations circulate their ideas in weekly meeting.

Table 88: Do you create environment to delegate decision making to the lowest level possible?

Option	Frequency	Percent
Yes	26	52.0
No	24	48.0
Total	50	100.0

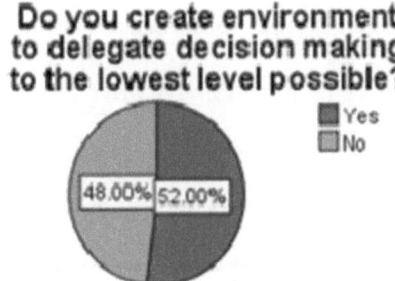

Figure 100: Do you create environment to delegate decision making to the lowest level possible?

Communication is prime factor for any organization. The need for open communication, freedom to express ideas and providing platform to employees to express new ideas can not only increases creativity but also increases the confidence of employees. Employees feel happy as they are empowered to be a part of planning of organization. Nearly 84% organizations have open communication at work place. Nearly 92% organizations capture the creative insight of employees by soliciting their ideas for improvement while 84% organizations provide any platform to present their ideas. And 46% of the organizations circulate their ideas in meeting. While 52% organizations create environment to delegate decision making to the lowest level possible.

Other facilities for employee

Table 89: Does the organization provide canteen facilities to the employees?

Option	Frequency	Percent
Yes	37	74.0
No	13	26.0
Total	50	100.0

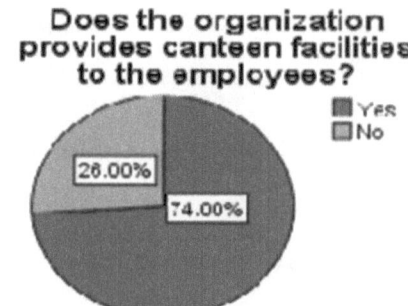

Figure 101: Does the organization provide canteen facilities to the employees?

Nearly 74% organisations provide canteen facilities to employees.

Table 90: Does the organization provide medical facilities to employees?

option	No. of employees	Percentage
Yes	50	100.0

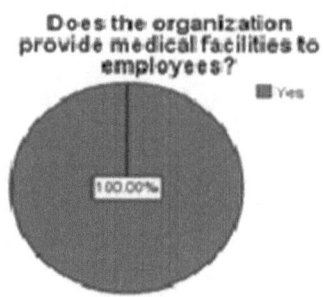

Figure 102: Does the organization provide medical facilities to employees?

All the organisations provide medical facilities to employees.

Table 91: Does the organization provide medical facilities to employee's family?

option	No. of employees	Percentage
Yes	48	96.0
No	2	4.0
Total	50	100.0

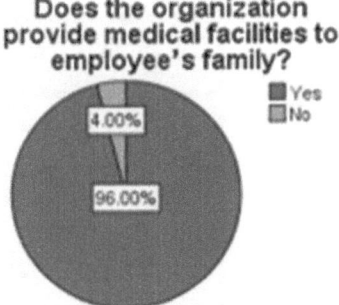

Figure 103: Does the organization provide medical facilities to employee's family?

Nearly 96% organisations provide medical facilities for their families.

Table 92: Does the organization provide financial help for employee's child education?

option	No. of employees	Percentage
Yes	21	42.0
No	29	58.0
Total	50	100.0

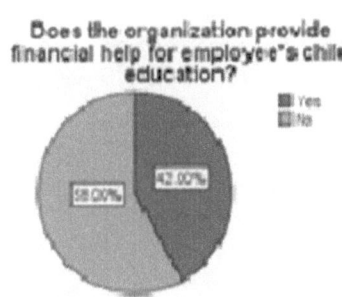

Figure 104: Does the organization provide financial help for employee's child education?

Only 42% organisations provide financial help for child education of employees.

Table 93: Does the organization provide financial/educational help to employees to upgrade their qualification?

option	No. of employees	Percentage
Yes	17	34.0
No	33	66.0
Total	50	100.0

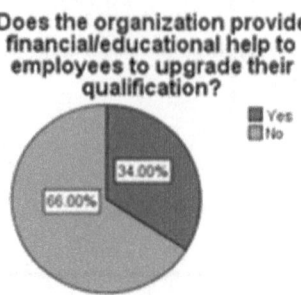

Figure 105: Does the organization provide financial/educational help to employees to upgrade their qualification?

Only 34% organisations provide financial/educational help to employees to upgrade their qualification.

Table 94: Does the organization carry survey to benchmark salary standards with the respective industry?

option	No. of employees	Percentage
Yes	35	70.0
No	15	30.0
Total	50	100.0

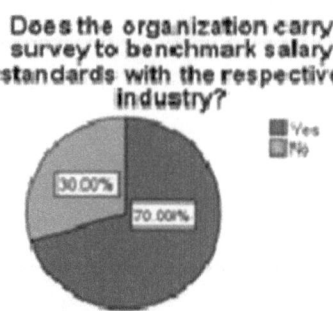

Figure 106: Does the organization carry survey to benchmark salary standards with the respective industry?

Table 95: Are the salary standards benchmarked with other organizations?

option	No. of employees	Percentage
Yes	38	76.0
No	12	24.0
Total	50	100.0

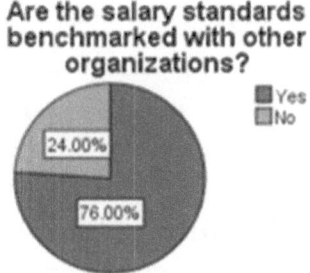

Figure 107: Are the salary standards benchmarked with other organizations?

Table 96: Does the management have vision for employee branding?

option	Frequency	Percent
Yes	6	12.0
No	44	88.0
Total	50	100.0

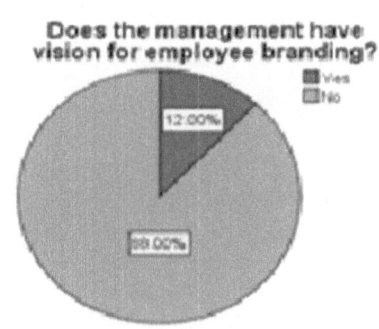

Figure 108: Does the management have vision for employee branding?

Table 97: Does the Organisation participate in employee branding competitions?

	No. of employees	Percentage
Yes	1	2.0
No	49	98.0
Total	50	100.0

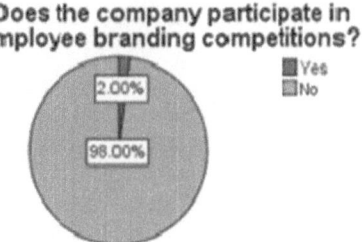

Figure 109: Does the Organisation participate in employee branding competitions?

When asked about other facilities provide to employees so as to have employee engagement and well-being of employees, 74% organizations provide canteen facilities. Nearly all organization provides medical facilities for employees while 96% provide medical facilities to their family. 42% organizations help financially for child education while only 33% organizations provide financial/educational help to employees to upgrade their qualification. 70% organizations carry survey to benchmark salary standards with the respective industry and their salary is standard benchmarked with industry. Only 12% managers have vision for employee branding while only 2% organisations participate in employee branding competitions.

CHAPTER 6

RESULTS AND DISCUSSION

A s India Inc has identified HR management as need of the organisation only around late 80's era, its various functions are still at the stage of growing importance so its variables and drivers & their significance in driving organisational performance and growth.

Earlier researches have done progressive work and established that employee performance is not alone based & depend upon his knowledge base, individual's capability, familiarity with new technology etc but other factors like:

- ❖ Pay & allowances
- ❖ Rewards & recognitions
- ❖ Work life balance
- ❖ Treatment employees are getting from the supervisors
- ❖ Performance management system
- ❖ Work environment of the organization

Further studies established above factors and few others consolidating as "Employee Satisfaction" as major factor effecting employee performance and also that apart from other business decisions and functions employee performance too plays important role in "Organisational performance".

Researchers pushed the momentum in identifying clear and definable constituents that are directly/indirectly effect "Organisational performance" as under:

- ❖ Turn over
- ❖ Customer base
- ❖ Manufacturing Costs
- ❖ Employee Cost
- ❖ Profit & loss

As the market moved on from monopolistic scenario to competitive market it posed threats to sustenance of the organisation resulting into closure of many small and medium sized industries and Organisational performance found few new constituents changing the whole philosophy of business from running a business to business management giving initially shifting focus from just production cost & profitability to new components as essential functions for sustained Business, recasting definition of "Organisational performance" as under:

- ❖ Vision & Mission strategy of Organisation
- ❖ Organisational goals
- ❖ Productivity
- ❖ Quality for Customer satisfaction
- ❖ Employee satisfaction
- ❖ Employee performance
- ❖ Profitability

Upon reaching practical definition of "Organisational Performance" industry and researchers started studying identifying components and drivers of "Employee Satisfaction" as under:

Components of Employee Satisfaction

- ❖ Job role clarity
- ❖ Treatment by supervisors

- ❖ Salary and allowances
- ❖ Knowledge and Career development
- ❖ Reward & recognition

Drivers to Employee Satisfaction

- ❖ Work culture
- ❖ People management practices
- ❖ Compensation & other benefits
- ❖ Career growth opportunities
- ❖ Systems & Procedures
- ❖ Quality of life

Studies further suggested that despite usually having good count of long term employees, with the market competition becoming fierce, retention of employee became a big challenge for India Inc.

Industry's internal surveys, academic researchers and management consultants established that Employee engagement is one of the major factor which was resultant of Employee satisfaction, which ensures employees to continue with the organisation for long term.

Further studies revealed that though components and drivers of employee engagement are very closely associated but there was need to recast few components and add few more components to achieve competitive Employee engagement, such as:

- ❖ Policies & practices: Organisation Practices requiring to be more diverse in terms of from just HR policies & practices to all the Policies to be bench marked with the market scenario.
- ❖ People: Base of people need to be broadened to include direct/indirect customers along with employees and its management policies too.

❖ Autonomy & Empowerment: As per experience & capability while discharging their duty Employees must be given autonomy and empowered to take decision.

Researches indicate that the Employee engagement results into "Employee Well-being" which includes Psychological and Physical well-being and its drivers as under:

❖ Personal effects

❖ Work culture

❖ Work environment

However, previous Studies couldn't identify & establish significant & clear definition and relationship between Employee engagement, Employee Well-being, Organisational culture and Organisational Performance.

This Study has used the Employee's input data of existing employee engagement level of targeted manufacturing industries to analyze and define employee engagement and Employee well-being criteria which effect Organisational performance through employee performance.

The Data collected was analysed using SPSS version 20 and following were the extracted:

General view

Out of 600 blue collared employees 366 are male and 234 are females. The male: female ratio is 61:31. While for white collared employees, 390 males and 210 females participated in the survey ranging from 21 yrs to 55 yrs of age group.

The mean age of employees of both White and Blue collared employees is between 26 to 35 years.

The mean experience for white collared employees in the Organization is 2 years to 3 years while for blue collared employees it is 6 years to 10 years.

White collared employees/executives and managers tend to switch their job frequently i.e. in 2 to 3 years while most of the stick to one Organization i.e. more than 4 yrs which is 32% of all employees. This indicates that they are loyal to Organization because of reasons i.e job satisfaction, employee engagement and other policies which are in benefit of employees.

It is important to note that the employees tend to remain in same Organisation for most of the time of their work tenure as the work allotted to them is specific and they are trained for the same within the given time period and hence they are happy, satisfied and loyal to the Organization.

Organisation Leadership and Planning

This is important to know that how much employees are aware of the organization and how much they believe in organization. This depicts the open culture of organization which helps employees to live freely in organization while working on their goals.

White collared employees, out of 600 employees 80.8% feel satisfied while working with the organization and in case of blue collared employees 77.8% employees feel satisfied. Feeling satisfied while working for the organization is important because it indicates the employees' basic needs are being fulfilled and they are happy with the rules and regulations and the policies of the organization.

41% of the white collared employees knew the organization goals and objective while nearly 59% does not know about it. This questions was specifically asked to white collared employees only as they are engaged mostly in office/desk work and the hierarchy is mostly well defined in the organizations and so every employee is told his key areas of responsibilities which are in alignment with the organization goal. It also shows how employees are engaged in Organisation goal with his/her personal goal.

Employees were also quizzed about the leadership in organization, whether employees trust their leadership and do the leaders live up to the core value of organization. This was important question from the organization point of view as it depicts the leadership is well managed and widely accepted by all the employees and they are happy with their senior leaders and would like to work under them and would like to refer the leaders as their role model. It not only will increase their efficiency but also their trust level towards leaders and organization too. Ultimately it will result in healthy relationship between Leaders and employees and will help in maintaining the wellbeing of employees, i.e. psychological well-being. It will ultimately result in increase in organization performance. 75% of Blue collared employees have confidence in their organization leaders while 78% of the Blue collared employees are happy with the organization while rest are unhappy.

40% Blue collared employees replied "very often" while 31% said "often" that leaders in the organization are ready to accept the inputs. Hence, in most of the organizations seniors accept the input from employees.

Nearly 70% Blue collared employees agreed that their leaders live the core value and so they can act as a role model for others, 56% Blue collared employees have clear understanding of their job while 44% does not have it.

80% White collared employees were satisfied with the organization while 41% people knew about the organization goal. It is an important component for organisational performance and can be of concern as individual goal is derived from organization goal.

92% White collared employees people have confidence in leadership and it is a positive factor, 87% people think that their managers live up to the core value of organization. 83% White collared employees think that managers are ready to accept the inputs from employees.

85% White collared employees think that there is open and detailed communication in the organization which is very important driver for employee engagement. 63% White collared employees think that they get all the necessary office equipments essential to do their duty at work place.

Combined Effects

When studied "Combined effects" of responses received from the White and Blue collared employees 80% of both employees are happy with organization which shows that they like the organization and also the job. Nearly 84% employees have confidence in the leadership of organization. They look up to them as a guide and mentor to improve in their work and trust them.

85% employees think the leaders live up to core values of the organization which indicates that they are committed to Organisational value system. It helps in increasing the confidence of employees in the leaders.

When the employees are given freedom to take decision for their work, they not only feel empowered but also involve in the task in detail and use their full potential to complete the given task. Giving them platform to express their ideas or accepting their inputs for improvement of work not only give them recognition (Social need- Maslow's Hierarchy of needs) but also increase their confident (self-esteem – Maslow's hierarchy of needs). When these needs are fulfilled employees are bound to engage at the workplace and use their optimum potential to complete their task.

The free flow of communication especially communication from Management to Employees in the organization plays vital role in achieving employee engagement and thereby employee well-being. The transparent vertical communication is very important as it reduces the gap between senior management and employees. Employees can approach senior management for resolving their issues and for guidance to achieve their goals. It not only keeps them happy and involved in the work they do but also psychologically satisfied and content for their work.

Organization culture and work environment

The organization culture and work environment at the work place plays a vital role in employee engagement and so the well-being. Work environment is very significant while studying the engagement and well-being as it not only indicates how employees feel safe and secure in the organization.

The work place climate in most industries is very unsafe and in pathetic condition due to lack of proper ventilation, improper/insufficient lighting, unsafe drinking water, polluted air due to dust/fumes, high decibel noise, poor state of office structure and equipment provided to employees to execute tasks etc. Further, these organisations despite knowing these organisation lack basic fire & industrial safety equipments/personal safety equipments, emergency services, health services etc. These factors have direct impact on employee's engagement levels and performance as well.

In the recent past there has been a revolutionary change in the approach in the employer's attitude wherein they have started taking these hazards seriously and mitigating with professional approach. Most organisations now have very motivating policies such as Environment, Health & Safety polices in place with lot of emphasis health & safety of employees while at work place. Apart from these employers have also introduced motivational schemes such as Performance based incentives, Variable pay, flexi timing, maternity & paternity leaves to maintain work life balance etc.

Organisations also have taken initiative to connect with the employees directly through exclusive communication channel sharing organisational information. To help employees improve their performance and also add up new skills In addition to motivation, employees need the skills and ability to do their job effectively. And for many organisations, training the employee has become a necessary input into the production process.

Quality of product for customer satisfaction is necessary has been responded by 50.5% employees. 57.2% employees responded that good co-operation among the seniors; peers and subordinates exist in their organisations as one of the major factor contributing to organisational culture & work environment. Results show that conducive work environment exists and maintained which help them perform their job comfortably. Overall 60% employees are happy with the work environment.

In response to questions asked about their perception about the job assigned to them and their connection to leaders 64.35% employees said that their seniors are easily approachable. 42.9% employees said that they have freedom to express their opinion without any negative consequences. 50% employees trust their supervisor, 64.35% employees like their job and feel their job is secure. 71.5% employees think that their job matches with their skills and knowledge helping them complete their job effectively. 64.35% employees feel that organization respect & value them as effective employee.

Factor analysis

Factor analysis is a methodology for Data reduction using unobservable variables found in the observed variables (manifest variables).

While using SPSS 20 Matrix of observed variables are drawn and matched for correlation; matrix which are within acceptable & close proximity range are retained and rest dumped.

There are many different methods to conduct "Factor Analysis" such as:

a. Principal axis factor
b. Maximum likelihood
c. Generalized least squares
d. Unweighted least squares

After initial extraction of factors many types of rotations can be done, e.g. **Orthogonal rotations**:

a. Varimax and
b. Equimax,
   Both types of rotations enforce restriction "factors cannot be correlated".

   Oblique rotations, such as
c. Promax, which allow the factors to be correlated with one another.

There are number of factors determined that need to be extracted. Using various factor analytic techniques and options, analysts can obtain results analyzing same data set. However, all analysts depend upon **Simple structure**, which is a pattern of results that each variable loads highly onto only one factor.

Factor analysis technique requires data from large sample size. Factor analysis is based on the correlation matrix of the variables involved, and correlations usually need a large sample size before they stabilize. Famous Researchers Tabachnick & Fidell, cite Comrey & Lee's advise sample size as under:

a. 50 cases –Very poor
b. 100 cases – Poor
c. 200 cases – Fair
d. 300 cases – Good
e. 500 cases – Very good, and
f. 1000 or more – Excellent.

Minimum 10 observations per variable are essential to escape computational hitches.

In this Study Data collected for the research was put through SPSS 20 to draw correlation matrix to identify major variables. Factor analysis has been done to identify the major variables for the employee engagement.

White collared employees

At the first instance, results are as follows:

Component Matrix (WCE)

1. Trust level of organisation

   Component 1: 0.702

   Component 2: -0.426

2. Quality of product for customer satisfaction.

   Component 1: 0.744

   Component 2: 0.288

3. Co-operation among the seniors, peers and subordinates.

   Component 1: 0.692

   Component 2: 0.292

4. Safety measures taken by organization.

   Component 1: 0.787

   Component 2: -0.172

5. Physical working conditions.

   Component 1: 0.716

   Component 2: -0.280

6. Temperature of work place.

   Component 1: 0.734

   Component 2: -0.053

7. Noise control at work place.

   Component 1: 0.707

   Component 2: -0.085

8. Are the seniors easily approachable?

Component 1: 0.629

Component 2: 0.259

9. Do you have a freedom to express your opinion without any negative consequences?

Component 1: 0.632

Component 2: 0.313

10. Do you feel that you can trust your supervisor?

Component 1: 0.710

Component 2: 0.025

11. Do you like your job ?

Component 1:: 0.722

Component 2: 0.271

12. Do you think that your job is secure?

Component 1: 0.682

Component 2: 0.097

13. How do you rate your present job with the skill set you have?

Component 1: 0.663

Component 2: 0.425

14. How will you rate organisation's respect and value towards you?

Component 1: 0.667

Component 2: 0.341

Extraction Method: Principal Component Analysis.

After removing the factors which are rated below 7 are removed from the list and again factor analysis done. The result is as follows:

Component Matrix final

1. Trust level of organisation

Component 1: 0.765

2. Quality of product for customer satisfaction.
Component 1: 0.787

3. Co-operation among the seniors, peers and subordinates.
Component 1: 0.735

4. Safety measures taken by organization.
Component 1: 0.821

5. Physical working conditions.
Component 1: 0.756

6. Temperature of work place.
Component 1: 0.744

7. Noise control at work place.
Component 1: 0.714

8. Do you feel that you can trust your supervisor?
Component 1: 0.705

Extraction Method: Principal Component Analysis.

a. 01 components extracted.

The above are the main variables which directly affect the employee engagement for white collared employees.

Blue Collared Employees

Results of Factor analysis for blue collared employees are as under:

Component Matrix (BCE)

1. Trust level of organisation.
Component 1: 0.718
Component 2: 0.016
Component 3: -0.087

2. Quality of product for customer satisfaction.
Component 1: 0.627
Component 2: -0.185
Component 3: 0.223

3. Co-operation among the seniors peers and subordinates.

    Component 1: 0.730

    Component 2: 0.089

    Component 3: -0.226

4. Safety measures taken by organization

    Component 1: 0.660

    Component 2: -0.330

    Component 3: 0.322

5. Physical working conditions.

    Component 1: 0.588

    Component 2: 0.340

    Component 3: -0.226

6. Temperature of work place.

    Component 1: 0.616

    Component 2: -0.484

    Component 3: 0.291

7. Noise control at work place

    Component 1: 0.588

    Component 2: 0.500

    Component 3: -0.258

8. Regular inspection of the plant and machinery to avoid the hazards organised by organization.

    Component 1: 0.541

    Component 2: -0.466

    Component 3: 0.147

9. Are the seniors easily approachable?

    Component 1: 0.597

    Component 2: 0.435

    Component 3: 0.145

10. Do you have a freedom to express your opinion without any negative consequences?

Component 1: 0.513

Component 2: -0.467

Component 3: -0.311

11. Do you feel that you can trust your supervisor?

Component 1: 0.495

Component 2: 0.421

Component 3: 0.472

12. Do you like your job ?

Component 1: 0.496

Component 2: -0.170

Component 3: -0.470

13. Do you think that your job is secure?

Component 1: 0.451

Component 2: 0.266

Component 3: 0.456

14. How do you rate your present job with the skill set you have?

Component 1: 0.441

Component 2: 0.067

Component 3: -0.230

15. How will you rate organisation's respect and value towards you?

Component 1: 0.541

Component 2: 0.037

Component 3: -0.240

Extraction Method: Principal Component Analysis.

a. 03 components extracted.

After removing the factors which are rated below 7 are removed from the list and again factor analysis done. The result is as follows,

Component Matrix final

1. Trust level of organisation
   Component 1: 0.765
2. Quality of product for customer satisfaction.
   Component 1: 0.787
3. Co-operation among the seniors, peers and subordinates.
   Component 1: 0.735
4. Safety measures taken by organization.
   Component 1: 0.821
5. Physical working conditions.
   Component 1: 0.756
6. Temperature of work place.
   Component 1: 0.744
7. Noise control at work place.
   Component 1: 0.744
8. Do you feel that you can trust your supervisor?
   Component 1: 0.705

   Extraction Method: Principal Component Analysis.

   a. 1 Components extracted.

The above are the main variables which directly affect the employee engagement for white collared employees.

Employee engagement factors I

In this series of Questions below mentioned% of Respondents have replied in "Affirmative".

Organization Culture

1. Trust level of organization
   Blue Collared Employees: 28.90%
   White Collared Employees: 14.30%
   Combined Effect: 21.60%

2. Quality of product for customer satisfaction.
   Blue Collared Employees: 50.05%
   White Collared Employees: 50.05%
   Combined Effect: 50.05%

3. Co-operation among the seniors peers and subordinates.
   Blue Collared Employees: 64.35%
   White Collared Employees: 50.05%
   Combined Effect: 57.20%

Work environment

4. Safety measures taken by organization.
   Blue Collared Employees: 35.75%
   White Collared Employees: 57.20%
   Combined Effect: 46.47%

5. Physical working conditions.
   Blue Collared Employees: 57.20%
   White Collared Employees: 57.20%
   Combined Effect: 57.20%

6. Temperature of work place.
   Blue Collared Employees: 64.35%
   White Collared Employees: 64.35%
   Combined Effect: 64.35%

7. Noise control at work place.
   Blue Collared Employees: 64.35%
   White Collared Employees: 71.50%
   Combined Effect: 67.92%

8. Regular inspection of the plant and machinery to avoid the hazards organized by organization.
   Blue Collared Employees: 71.50%
   White Collared Employees: 71.50%
   Combined Effect: 71.50%

9. Are the seniors easily approachable?

   Blue Collared Employees: 71.50%

   White Collared Employees: 57.20%

   Combined Effect: 64.35%

10. Do you have a freedom to express your opinion without any negative consequences?

    Blue Collared Employees: 28.60%

    White Collared Employees: 57.20%

    Combined Effect: 42.90%

WORK IN THE ORGANIZATION

1. Do you feel that you can trust your supervisor?

   Blue Collared Employees: 42.90%

   White Collared Employees: 57.20%

   Combined Effect: 50.05%

2. Do you like your job ?

   Blue Collared Employees: 71.50%

   White Collared Employees: 57.20%

   Combined Effect: 64.35%

3. Do you think that your job is secure?

   Blue Collared Employees: 71.50%

   White Collared Employees: 57.20%

   Combined Effect: 64.35%

4. How do you rate your present job with the skill set you have?

   Blue Collared Employees: 71.50%

   White Collared Employees: 71.50%

   Combined Effect: 71.50%

5. How will you rate organization's respect and value towards you?

   Blue Collared Employees: 71.50%

   White Collared Employees: 57.20%

   Combined Effect: 64.35%

The factors related to work culture; work environment and the relationship with the employees surrounding you in organization play a crucial role in employee engagement.

On being asked about Trust level nearly 28.9 Blue collared and 14.3 white collared employees answers affirmatively, while for Quality of product for customer satisfaction is better and is agreed by nearly 50.5% of the employees. Nearly 57.2% of all the employees think there is better co-operation among the seniors, peers and subordinates. Responding to work environment they responded that overall the work environment is properly maintained and they can perform their work comfortably in the environment. Overall 60% employees are happy with the work environment.

On being asked about their perception about the job they are doing and their surroundings 64.35% employees said that their seniors are easily approachable, 42.9 employees said that they have freedom to express their opinion without any negative consequences, 50% employees trust their supervisor, 64.35 employees like their job and feel their job is secure, 71.5% employees think that their job matches with their skills and knowledge so they can complete their job effectively, 64.35% employees feel that organization respect them value them as its effective employee.

Employee engagement factors II

In this series of Questions following% of Respondents have replied in "Yes"

1. Have you been treated well by the managers?

   Blue Collared Employees: 80%

   White Collared Employees: 80%

   Total no of Employees: 80%

2. Does your supervisor/manager handle your work related issue satisfactorily?

   Blue Collared Employees: 75%

White Collared Employees: 75%

Total no of Employees: 75%

3. Does your supervisor/manager tell when you do your job well?

   Blue Collared Employees: 75%

   White Collared Employees: 75%

   Total no of Employees: 75%

4. Does your supervisor/manager tell when you need any improvement?

   Blue Collared Employees: 75%

   White Collared Employees: 75%

   Total no of Employees: 75%

5. Do you like to go to job every day?

   Blue Collared Employees: 75%

   White Collared Employees: 75%

   Total no of Employees: 75%

The above factors indicate that how employees are treated in the organization, by their immediate managers and senior managers. It is directly related to the employee's psychological well-being as it may boost the employee to work better or can have negative impact if he will not get proper treatment by his seniors. As seen above employees are happy working with organisation as they being treated well by their managers, they are told when they do their job well and when they need improvement in work. 75% Employees like their job and wants to go to job every day.

Training and development

Responses received from employees indicate that 76% Blue collared employees and 64.5% White collared employees are happy and satisfied with the training given to them at the induction level. 38.5% White collared employees are completely happy with the tool and techniques used for training. 55% Blue collared employees and 47.50% White collared employees felt connected to the trainer as well as the content of training program. 69% Blue collared employees and 68% White collared employees would like to undergo T & D program for the betterment of their job and feel that this will help them improve their performance and help them to grow in their career. Most of the organizations provide training out of which 61% on job while 21% in classroom and some of the organizations provide both types of training.

75% "Blue collared" employees responded that they get training whenever necessary. 13% employees are totally satisfied while 41% are almost satisfied. 14% employees think they are completely connected to trainer while 55% think they are connected to an extent to trainer. 69% employees would like to undergo training programs to improve their performance. 12% employees feel that it will help them improve their performance definitely while 62% employees also think positively about it. 75% employees think that organizations provide them training whenever necessary.

64% "White collared" employees feel that organization provide training whenever necessary. 38% employees are satisfied completely while 15% are satisfied to an extent with the tools and techniques. Nearly 55% employees feel connected to trainer. 67% employees would like to undergo training to improve their performance. 37% employees feel that training program would definitely help them perform better in job, while 16% feel it can help them perform better in the job. 60% employees think that training given by organization will help them for career development and promotions too.

Combined Effect

69% employees of White & Blue collared feel that organization provides training whenever necessary. 20% employees feel totally while 29% feel almost satisfied with the training provided to them. 25% employee feel totally connected while 35% feel connected to trainer to an extent. 68% would like to undergo training and development to improve their work. It shows that they are eager to engage in the given job. 25% employees definitely think that training program will help them perform better on the job, and 39% employees think it can help them. 61% employees think that T & D given by the Organization help them for career development/promotions.

The above responses indicate that Training & Development is very important driver for Employee engagement, employee well-being, employee performance resulting into organisational performance.

Performance management

Nearly 55% "Blue collared" employees are not satisfied with the current appraisal process of their organization and they want to get it changed. Some have given suggestion to change in the increment system and basic salary structure. 67.5% employees are satisfied with promotional policies of the organization. Only 37% employees are happy with the current appraisal process which is issue of concern. 67% employees are happy with the promotional policies of organization.

84.67% "White collared" employees get JD and KRAs defined for the year. Nearly 88.83 employees think that PMS cover the key areas that focus on their expected performance area and professional growth.

The recognition is based 57% on seniority level and 39.50% on performance level. 72% white collared employees are happy with the promotional policies of the organization and 78.33% employees are happy with reward and recognition policies. 84% white collared employees think that organisation define their JD and KRAs properly. So they are aware about their duties and responsibilities. 89% employees think that PMS cover the key areas that focus on their personal development. 39% employees think that recognitions are based on performance, while 57% employees think that it is based on seniority. 72% white collared employees are happy with the promotional policies of the organization. 78% white collared employees are happy with the reward and recognition policies.

Combined Effect

Nearly 37% White & Blue collared employees are satisfied with the current performance appraisal process. Nearly 70% employees are happy with the promotional policies of the organization

Nearly half of the Blue collared employees would like work with same organization for more than 2 years. While for White collared employees the mean years for future working are 1 to 2 years. 57% of Blue collared employees and 52.3% White collared employees would like to recommend their friends or relatives the respective organization for work. 65.5% blue collared employees and 54% white collared employees would like to work extra to achieve the goal of the organization.

Responding a Question as to offer some suggestion to change the employee engagement policies, 96% both blue collared and White collared employees refused to offer any suggestion. It points to the fact that they are happy with the most of the HR policies of the organization.

Nearly 22% Blue collard employees would like to work for 1 year, 44% for 2 years and 28% for 3 years. This shows their loyalty to the organization. 57% employees would like to recommend their friends and relatives the organization. 65% employees would like to give extra efforts for the organization. This shows their loyalty to the organization.

3% White collard employees would like to suggest improving satisfaction level in organization which shows that employees are satisfied in the organization.

HR Managers

This study also collected & analysed response data through Questionnaire from HR managers to understand effectiveness and relevance of HR Policies to Organisational objectives and goals of Employee engagement, employee well-being, employee performance and organisational performance.

HR Managers were asked Questions about the different employee engagement policies of the organization, the overall work culture of the organization, work environment and the salary, Rewards and recognition policies as well as annual meetings, and get together for employees family.

HR managers were also asked Questions about the succession plan of the organization. For which positions the succession plan is done and what are the percentages of management levels are at place. Data shows that the mean percentage is 48.68% while median is 50% and mode is 80% with std. Deviation 30.27%.

While responding to Questions about the recruitment for vacated or new positions, if it is done through lateral entry or internal up gradation. The responses were, mean 80.66% was through lateral entry with median 80%, mode 80% and std. Deviation 13.86%. Similarly the internal promotions/hiring responses were, mean 19.34%, median 20%, mode 20% with std. Deviation 13.86.

Responses of HR managers indicated that the HR policies of Organisation, Training programs, Performance management system, other facilities, compensation and employee branding are directly related to employee engagement and so the employee wellbeing, employee & organisational performance.

Responses of HR managers revealed that 86% organisations have manpower plan and 72% of the organisations have mapped competency for every position.

Response data on staff turnover record indicated that 94% HR managers told that their organization monitor the attrition trends. While 66% people say that their Employee welfare schemes help retain employees like salary hike, good welfare activities, working environment, suggestion box, Gratuity, superannuation, group medi-claim, compensation and benefits

- short term and long term, retention bonus, talent mapping, stock options only for GM level. 92% of the organisation's HR policies help employee retention.

Responding upon "Training & Development" activity HR managers indicated that 86% of the organisations have clear training plan for the employees. 80% of the organisations ask feedback about the training and development programme. HR Managers of 86% organizations informed about having strategically well-structured Training & Development Policy and Calendar.

All the organizations unanimously agree that the employees are benefited by training and development programs conducted by organization. Training and development is important part of engagement as it leads to better job performance, better career and so better well-being and satisfied employee.

HR managers indicated that various performance management systems are in use. Most commonly used are Bell curve, 360 degree feedback, PMS and MBO systems. 74% organizations give constructive feedback to increase employee's performance so as to increase performance of the employees. 46% organizations include customer satisfaction as one of the criteria for performance appraisal which 54% organizations do not agree with it. Nearly 40% organizations carry the feedback survey for employees to measure the impact of HR policies and employee engagement programs on their performance.

Responding to Questions on various other drivers for employee engagement 89% organisations have open communication environment, 92% organisations have vision for the creativity of employees and they solicit their ideas. 84% organisations provide employees a platform to present their ideas.

74% organisations provide canteen facilities to employees. 96% organisations provide medical facilities for their families. 42% organisations provide financial help for child education of employees. 34% organisations provide financial/educational help to employees to upgrade their qualification. 70% organizations carry survey to benchmark salary standards with the respective industry and their salary is standard benchmarked with industry. 12% managers have vision for employee branding while only 2% organisations participate in employee branding competitions.

The study establishes the direct connection between employee engagement and organization culture and organization performance. For blue collared employees r value = 0.732 while for white collared employees r value = 0.709. It proves that employee engagement is crucial for job satisfaction, and employee loyalty and retention in the organization.

The Study further establishes connections between:

❖ Employee engagement and well-being criteria

❖ Impacts of Organisational culture on Employee engagement and Employee Well-being and

❖ Ultimately impacts of Employee engagement and Employee Well-being on Employee performance resulting into Organizational performance (in terms of productivity and profitability)

In order to carry out research to achieve above a Questionnaire was put through respondents out of Blue collared employees, White collared employees and HR Managers. Based on inputs received from Questionnaire Independent and Dependent variables were identified as shown in the below:

Independent Variables

❖ Physical work environment

❖ Work life balance

❖ Psychological well-being

❖ Autonomy

❖ Relationship with co-employees and senior management.

❖ Medical facilities given to employees and their family

❖ Canteen facilities provided

- ❖ Training and development
- ❖ Career opportunities
- ❖ Rewards and recognition
- ❖ Pay and benefits
- ❖ Senior leadership
- ❖ Co-employees, team work

Dependent variables

- ❖ Job satisfaction
- ❖ Job involvement
- ❖ Sense of accomplishment
- ❖ Well-being of employees
- ❖ Individual performance
- ❖ Organization performance

The Study revealed that Employee well-being need not be either due to Employee engagement objectives of the organisation or connected to the organisational culture, as this can be also due to limited personal needs and low esteem of the employee such as:

- ❖ Distance between office and home
- ❖ Lack of ambition for career growth
- ❖ Stable job even if lower salary
- ❖ Salary drawn enough for survival and meet family needs etc

The study also revealed that not all engaged employees contribute to the organisational performance as many employees can be found engaged as long as they feel their job is safe and also those feel their past performance during the initial growth of the organisation is good enough to protect their jobs.

Similarly study also reveals that most blue collared and even reasonable number of white collared employees found to be engaged though not experiencing well-being level at satisfactory scale but just because they donot wish to migrate to out of state for job.

The study established that Organisation culture is very essential component for achieving:

- ❖ High employee morale
- ❖ Consistent, efficient employee performance
- ❖ Team cohesiveness
- ❖ Competitive edge derived from innovation and customer service
- ❖ Strong organisational alignment & commitment towards goal achievement

The study further reveals that the Organisational culture is great contributor to achieving and enhancing Employee engagement and thereby Employee Well-being levels in an organisation.

The study established components of Organisational culture as under:

- ❖ Vision and Mission
- ❖ Core Values of the organisation
- ❖ Camaraderie spirit among employees
- ❖ Celebrations for the success attained by team
- ❖ Community services for society
- ❖ Communication with employees a regular practice
- ❖ Caring approach to employees
- ❖ Commitment to ensure Learning for employees
- ❖ Consistency in well-established practices
- ❖ Connect with people
- ❖ Chronicles

The Study established that most organisations faced with high attritions are those with low employee engagement scores thereby low employee well-being counts. The study further established that an engagement practice of an organisation enhances employee well-being which improves employee retention rate by reducing attrition.

The study reveals the direct connection between employee well-being through employee engagement and its impact on organization performance. It proves that employee engagement is crucial for job satisfaction, well-being of employee and employee loyalty and retention in the organization ultimately for the organisational performance.

The factors which are important in employee engagement and well-being of the employees are found from this research which are termed as "Drivers of employee engagement" as under:

- ❖ Work
- ❖ People
- ❖ Opportunities
- ❖ Total Rewards
- ❖ Organisation Practices
- ❖ Quality of Life

These factors play important role in physical and psychological well-being of the employees and so the employee engagement. When employees are happy and engaged in the organization, they like their work and use full potential to complete the given task. When they are efficient and effective it directly results into increased productivity and profitability. When Employees are happy and contented, it increases their morale, motivation and loyalty to the organization. It ultimately results in employee retention and decreased attrition rate of organization.

Engaged employees play role in organization accomplish mission, execute its strategy and help organization to complete its mission. Engaged employees help organisations competitive advantages on account of enhanced productivity, better customer satisfaction and employee retention. Hence, employee engagement needs to be taken as a continuous process of learning, measurement, and improvement.

The relationship between employee engagement, well-being and organizational outcomes would be superior if better measures are used and employee feedback are received and given due cognisance. This help organisations comprehend impact of various factors employee engagement and well-being and accordingly concentrate on these to achieve strategic results and thereby improve overall organisational effectiveness.

The study established a Conceptualization Model which connects following out comes of the research:

- ❖ Employee engagement is an essential activity to achieve organisational goal
- ❖ Employee engagement improves employee well-being
- ❖ Employee well-being directly effects employee behaviour and performance
- ❖ Employee engagement can be enhanced objectively thereby employee well-being can be enhanced
- ❖ Organisational culture plays pivotal role in achieving and enhancing employee engagement & employee well-being
- ❖ Employee engagement and employee well-being breeds employee loyalty
- ❖ Employee engagement and employee well-being enhanced employee retention
- ❖ Employee engagement and employee well-being reduces attrition
- ❖ Employee engagement and employee well-being has direct impact on organisational performance
- ❖ Employee engagement enhances employee well-being but employee wellbeing can also be independent of employee engagement

Based on inputs from research a Conceptual model shown below was established which clearly exhibits various relations matrix between the independent and dependent variables established for the research.

Conceptualization of model

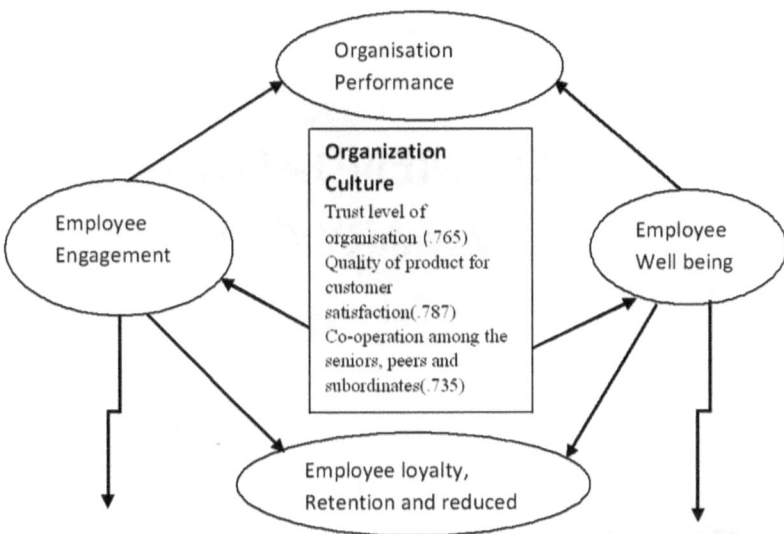

- Job involvement and liking for job (.722)
- organisation's respect and value towards Sense of accomplishment(.541)
- Career opportunities(.663)
- Rewards and recognition(.663)
- Trusting immediate boss(.705)
- Co-workers, team work and approachable seniors(.629)

- Physical work environment(.756)
- Work life balance and security of job (.682)
- Psychological well being and organisation's respect and value towards you(.667)
- Autonomy and freedom to express your opinion (.632)
- Relationship with co-workers and senior management(.735).
- Temperature and nose level in work environment (.734)

Figure 110: Conceptualization of model (Post Research)

CHAPTER 7

RECOMMENDATIONS & SUMMARY GAINS

SUMMARY GAINS

The study was conducted with very holistic objectives of finding out ways to enhance employee well-being through employee engagement strategies of the organisation and during the research it was found that employee engagement is not only a need of the organisation but also one of the major expectation of the employee across the board.

The study once adopted by the industry will have significant impact on the general levels of employee's psychology at the beginning and subsequently resulting into its enhanced performance.

The study establishes the direct connection between employee engagement and organization culture and organization performance. It also proves that employee engagement is crucial for job satisfaction, and employee loyalty and retention in the organization.

The Study further establishes connections between:

❖ Employee engagement and well-being criteria

- ❖ Impacts of Organisational culture on Employee engagement and Employee Well-being and
- ❖ Ultimately impacts of Employee engagement and Employee Well-being on Employee performance resulting into Organizational performance (in terms of productivity and profitability)

The Study also established:

Independent Variables

- ❖ Physical work environment
- ❖ Work life balance
- ❖ Psychological well-being
- ❖ Autonomy
- ❖ Relationship with co-employees and senior management.
- ❖ Medical facilities given to employees and their family
- ❖ Canteen facilities provided
- ❖ Training and development
- ❖ Career opportunities
- ❖ Rewards and recognition
- ❖ Pay and benefits
- ❖ Senior leadership
- ❖ Co-employees, team work

Dependent variables

- ❖ Job satisfaction
- ❖ Job involvement
- ❖ Sense of accomplishment
- ❖ Well-being of employees
- ❖ Individual performance
- ❖ Organization performance

The Study revealed that Employee well-being need not be either due to Employee engagement objectives of the organisation or connected to the organisational culture, as this can be also due to limited personal needs and low esteem of the employee such as:

- ❖ Distance between office and home
- ❖ Lack of ambition for career growth
- ❖ Stable job even if lower salary
- ❖ Salary drawn enough for survival and meet family needs etc

The study established that Organisation culture is very essential component for achieving:

- ❖ High employee morale
- ❖ Consistent, efficient employee performance
- ❖ Team cohesiveness
- ❖ Competitive edge derived from innovation and customer service
- ❖ Strong organisational alignment & commitment towards goal achievement

The study further reveals that the Organisational culture is great contributor to achieving and enhancing Employee engagement and thereby Employee Well-being levels in an organisation.

The study established components of Organisational culture as under:

- ❖ Vision and Mission
- ❖ Core Values of the organisation
- ❖ Camaraderie spirit among employees
- ❖ Celebrations for the success attained by team
- ❖ Community services for society
- ❖ Communication with employees a regular practice
- ❖ Caring approach to employees
- ❖ Commitment to ensure Learning for employees

- ❖ Consistency in well-established practices
- ❖ Connect with people
- ❖ Chronicles

The Study established that most organisations faced with high attritions are those with low employee engagement scores thereby low employee well-being counts. The study further established that engagement practices of an organisation enhances employee well-being which improves employee retention rate by reducing attrition.

The factors which are important in employee engagement and well-being of the employees are found from this research which are termed as "Drivers of employee engagement" as under:

- ❖ Work
- ❖ People
- ❖ Opportunities
- ❖ Total Rewards
- ❖ Organisation Practices
- ❖ Quality of Life

The relationship between employee engagement, well-being and organizational outcomes would be superior if better measures are used and employee feedback are received and given due cognisance. This help organisations comprehend impact of various factors employee engagement and well-being and accordingly concentrate on these to achieve strategic results and thereby improve overall organisational effectiveness.

Final Results

The above analysis of data and subsequent discussions offer final results of the research study as under:

a. **Assumption 1 (H1): Employee Engagement is not affected significantly by Employee Well being has been Rejected.**

b. **Assumption 2 (H2): Employee Engagement significantly affect Employee Performance has been Accepted.**

c. **Assumption 3 (H3): There is not any significant affect of Employee Engagement on Organisation Performance has been Rejected.**

The study established a Conceptualization Model which connects following out comes of the research:

❖ Employee engagement is an essential activity to achieve organisational goal

❖ Employee engagement improves employee well-being

❖ Employee well-being directly effects employee behaviour and performance

❖ Employee engagement can be enhanced objectively thereby employee well-being can be enhanced

❖ Organisational culture plays pivotal role in achieving and enhancing employee engagement & employee well-being

❖ Employee engagement and employee well-being breeds employee loyalty

❖ Employee engagement and employee well-being enhanced employee retention

❖ Employee engagement and employee well-being reduces attrition

❖ Employee engagement and employee well-being has direct impact on organisational performance

❖ Employee engagement enhances employee well-being but employee wellbeing can also be independent of employee engagement

Based on inputs from research a Conceptual model shown below was established which clearly exhibits various relations matrix between the independent and dependent variables established for the research.

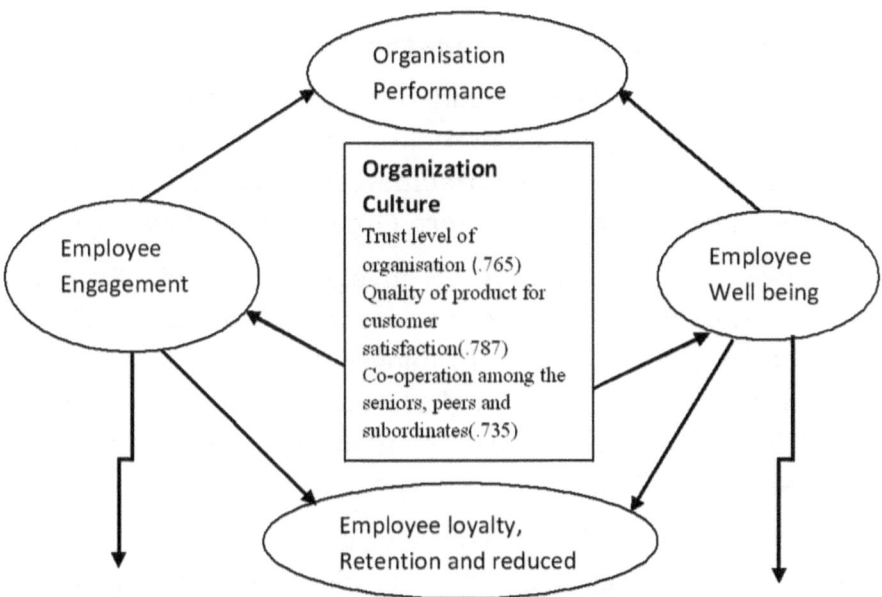

- Job involvement and liking for job (.722)
- organisation's respect and value towards Sense of accomplishment(.541)
- Career opportunities(.663)
- Rewards and recognition(.663)
- Trusting immediate boss(.705)
- Co-workers, team work and approachable seniors(.629)

- Physical work environment(.756)
- Work life balance and security of job (.682)
- Psychological well being and organisation's respect and value towards you(.667)
- Autonomy and freedom to express your opinion (.632)
- Relationship with co-workers and senior management(.735).
- Temperature and nose level in work environment (.734)

Figure 111: Conceptual Model (Post Research)

Recommendations

Recommendations to Top Management of the Industry

Based on Study it is recommended that Employee engagement, Employee well-being are theoretical terms but same should not adopted at universal scale to achieve its benefits in terms of Employee performance and in tern Organisational performance.

Components of Employee engagement and Employee wellbeing derived in the study are constant while Drivers Employee engagement and Employee wellbeing are variable in terms of their applicability/relevance would depend upon current levels of employee engagement & employee well-being and organisational culture.

In order to achieve employee well-being objectives which have direct bearing on organisational performance in achieving organisational goals, the Organisations are to conduct detailed survey components of employee well-being and current levels of employee engagement.

The Organisation's need to follow below process to make best use of the study and conceptual model:

    a. Carry out survey to study following:
        i.   Current levels of organisational culture:
        ii.   Current levels of employee engagement
        iii. Current levels of employee well-being
        iv. Relevant employee well-being components & its employee engagement drivers
        v.   Ways to improve employee engagement levels
        vi. Desired organisational culture needs

Once reference data for above factors are drawn from detailed employee survey, Top management in consultation with internal or external HR expert would need to draw strategy to achieve these. As the employee engagement levels and organisational culture levels improve, employee well-being levels with rise to the desired levels. These improvements will have direct impact on organisational performance towards achieving its business goals.

Once above process is complete organisational cultural and employee engagement part of HR policies would need recast, execution and continuous monitoring through regular formal and informal surveys for improvement in engagement &well-being levels and its impacts on employee performance and also organisational performance.

The organisation top management need to consider essentially that employee engagement and well-being are human process which is time consuming process and need continuous monitoring of its levels and also continuous aligning engagement section of HR policies.

Recommendations to HR Managers

HR manager is the Change agent for an Organisation, in order to use this model for the fullest benefit they are to bring revolutionary changes in the organisation in terms of updating Top Management, Senior Management, Middle Management and other grades of employees about:

a. The importance of employee engagement at all levels extending its impact in the form of employee well-being levels.

b. Impacts of employee engagements & employee well-being on individual and organisational performance.

c. Importance of surveys

d. Importance of giving unbiased inputs in survey with positive attitude

Once that is completed the HR managers should extract the data and interpret it for understanding needed:

a. Drivers for employee engagement,

b. Components of employee well-being,

c. Levels of organisational culture needed for enhanced employee engagement levels.

Once conclusive needs are extracted the HR manager must recast its employee engagement policy with cost implications and return of investment through its impact on enhanced organisational performance in terms of productivity and profitability.

HR managers should give a detailed presentation to the management on the strategy, its implementation, monitoring and mapping the impacts in terms of organisational performance.

HR manager must inculcate culture in the organisation for positive attitude towards honest response to surveys and help the organisation in achieving its goals.

Top Management and HR managers are to ensure that internal communication within the organisation which includes communication between management to employee in terms of vision & mission and employee to management in the form of regular employee engagement and employee satisfaction surveys becomes backbone of the organisation culture.

REFERENCES

Following Books, Articles, Research Papers, Web-sites etc were read by the Author while writing the book.

❖ A Research Paper on the Effect of Employee Engagement on Job Satisfaction in IT Sector, http://www.borjournals.com/a/index.php/jbmssr/article/viewFile/1685/1060 (Accessed on 23rd Jun 2014, at 23: 00 hrs)

❖ Ashton, C., & Morton, L. (2005).Managing talent for competitive advantage Strategic HR Review 4 (5), 28 –31.

❖ Apron, P (2008). Talent Management practices in selected companies listed on the stock exchange of Thailand. Educational Journal of Thailand. 2(1), 1-9.

❖ Abraham, S., 2012. Development of Employee Engagement Programme on the basis of Employee Satisfaction Survey. Journal of Economic Development, Management, IT, Finance and Marketing, 4(1), pp. 27-37.

❖ Advantage: HR's Strategic Role. HR Magazine, 52(3), Special section pp. 1-11.Springer Science+Business Media B.V. 2008 Ab

❖ Aktouf, O., 1992. Management and theories of organizations in the 1990s: Toward a critical radical humanism. Academy of Management Review, 17, pp. 407–431.

❖ Aspx (Accessed on 14th Feb 2014 at 21:00 hrs)

❖ Attridge, M., 2009. Measuring and Managing Employee Work Engagement: A Review of the Research and Business

Literature. Journal of Workplace Behavioral Health, 24(4), pp. 383 – 398.

❖ Bakker, A. and Schaufeli, W., 2008. Positive organizational behavior: Engaged employees in flourishing organizations. Journal of Organizational Behavior, 29, pp.147–154

❖ Bakker, A.B. and Demerouti, E., 2007. The job demands-resources model: state of the art. Journal of Managerial Psychology, 22(3), pp. 309–328.

❖ Bakker, A.B. and Demerouti, E., 2008. Towards a model of work engagement. Career Development International, 13(3), pp.209–223.

❖ Bakker, A.B. and Leiter M.P., 2010. Work engagement: a handbook of essential theory and research. New York, NY: Psychology Press.

❖ Bakker, A.B. and Leiter M.P., 2010. Work engagement: a handbook of essential theory and research. New York, NY: Psychology Press.

❖ Bakker, A.B., Hakanen, J.J., Demerouti, E. and Xanthopoulou, D., 2007. Job resources boost work engagement, particularly when job demands are high. Journal of Educational Psychology, 99(2), pp. 274-284.

❖ Balain S. and Sparrow P., 2009. Engaged to Perform: A new perspective on employee engagement: Executive Summary. Lancaster University Management School.

❖ Barsade, S., 2002. 'The ripple effect: emotional contagion and its influence on group behavior. Administrative Science Quarterly, 47, pp. 644-77.

❖ Best Practice in Promoting Employee Health and Wellbeing in the City of London

❖ Blumberg B., Cooper, D.R. and Schindler P.S., 2005. Business research methods. London: McGraw-Hill.

❖ Brian Becker, Barry Gerhart; The impact of human resources management on organisational performance : Process and

Prospects; Academy of Management Journal, 1996, vol 39, No 4, 779-801

❖ Bright, L., 2010. Why Age Matters in the Work Preferences of Public Employees: A Comparison of Three Age-Related Explanations. Public Personnel Management, 39(1), pp.1-14.

❖ Britt, T.W., Adler, A.B. and Bartone, P.T., 2001. Deriving benefits from stressful events: The role of engagement in meaningful work and hardiness. Journal of Occupational Health Psychology, 6(1), pp. 53-63.

❖ Buchanan, D., 1979. The Development of Job Design Theories and Techniques. New York: Praeger Publishers. Canadian Standards and Guidelines for Career Development Practitioners.

❖ Carley Foster, Khanyapuss Punjaisri, Ranis Cheng, (2010) "Exploring the relationship between corporate, internal and employer branding", Journal of Product & Brand Management, Vol. 19 Iss: 6, pp.401 – 409

❖ Cartwright, S. and Holmes, N., 2006. The meaning of work: the challenge of regaining employee engagement and reducing cynicism. Human Resource Management Review, 16, pp. 199–208.

❖ Causes and consequences of well-being 139 © 2009 The Author. Journal compilation © 2009 International Association of Applied Psychology.)

❖ Causes and Consequences†

❖ Chartered Institute of Personnel and Development (CIPD) (2006c) Working Life: Employee Attitudes and engagement 2006 Research Report

❖ Childs Julian H & Stoeber Joachim (2010) Self-Oriented, Other-Oriented and Socially Prescribed Perfectionism in Employees: Relationships with Burnout and Engagement. Journal of Workplace Behavioral Health, Vol. 25, Issue 4, p269-281

❖ Christian Homburg and Christian Pflesser, A multiple layer model of market oriented organisational culture : measurement issues and performance outcomes; Journal of Marketing Research, vol XXXVII (November 2000, 449-462)

❖ Corporate Leadership Council, 2002. Building the High-Performance Workforce A Quantitative Analysis of the Effectiveness of Performance Management Strategies, Washington, DC 60

❖ Creswell, J.W., 2009. Research design: qualitative, quantitative, and mixed methods approaches. 3rd ed. Thousand Oaks, Calif.: Sage Publications.

❖ Demerouti, E., Bakker, A.B., Nachreiner, F. and Schaufeli, W.B., 2001. The job demands-resources model of burnout. The Journal of applied psychology, 86(3), pp. 499 – 512.

❖ Denscombe, M., 2001. The good research guide: for small-scale social research projects. Buckingham: Open University Press.

❖ Dernovsek, D., 2008. Engaged Employees. Credit Union Magazine, 74(5), pp. 42.

❖ DeRue, D.S. and Morgeson, F.P., 2007. Stability and change in person-team and person-role fit over time: The effects of growth satisfaction, performance, and general self-efficacy. Journal of Applied Psychology. 92(5), pp. 1242-1253.

❖ education.qld.gov.au/health/docs/.../workplace-environment.doc (Accessed on 15th Jun 2014 at 23:30 hrs)

❖ Eisenberger, R., Huntington, R., Hutchison, S. and Sowa,D., 1986. Perceived organizational support. Journal of Applied Psychology, 71(3), pp. 500–507.

❖ Exploring employee engagement from the employee perspective: implications for HRD; Journal of European Industrial Training, Volume 35, Issue 4 (20110514), (Accessed on 25th Jul 2013, at 21:00 hrs)

❖ Felicia A Huppert*

❖ Fredrickson, B.L. and Joiner, T., 2002. Positive emotions trigger upward spirals toward emotional well-being. Psychological Science, 13, pp. 172-175.

❖ Fredrickson, B.L., 2001. The role of positive emotions in positive psychology: the broaden-and-build theory of positive emotions. American Psychologist,56, pp. 218-226.

❖ Frynas, J.G Millahi, K, & Pigman, G. A. (2006). First mover advantages in international business and firm-specific political resources, Strategic Management Journal, 27(4), 321-345.

❖ Gallup, 2006. Gallup study: engaged employees inspire Organisation innovation. The Gallup Management Journal. Available at: http://gmj.gallup.com/content/24880/ Gallup-Study-Engaged-Employees-Inspire-Organisation. aspx [Accessed 12 May 2012, at 21:45 hrs].

❖ Gallup, 2010, Employee engagement. What is your ration?. Available at: <http://www.gallup.com/consulting/121535/ employee-engagement-overview-brochure.aspx> [Accessed 20 February 2012 at 22:50 hrs].

❖ George, J. M., Reed, T. F., Ballard, K. A., Colin, J. And Fielding, J., 1993. Contact with AIDS patients as a source of work-related distress: Effects of organizational and social support. Academy of Management Journal, 36, 157–171.

❖ Ghauri, P. and Grønhaug, K., 2006. Research methods in business studies: a practical guide. 3rd ed. London: Ft Prentice Hall.

❖ Graen G.B., 2008. Enriched engagement through assistance to systems' change: a proposal. Industrial and Organizational Psychology, 1, pp. 74–75.

❖ Gravenkemper, S., 2007. Building Community in Organizations: Principles of Engagement. Consulting Psychology Journal: Practice and Research, 59(3), pp. 203-208.

* Grawitch, M.J., Gottschalk, M. and Munz, D.C., 2006. The path to a healthy workplace: A critical review linking healthy workplace practices, employee well-being, and organizational improvements. Consulting Psychology Journal: Practice and Research, 58(3), pp. 129 – 147.

* Greenberg, J., 1990. Organizational justice: Yesterday, today and tomorrow. Journal of Management, 16, pp. 399-432. 61

* Guest, D. (2006) Smarter ways of working – the benefits of and barriers to adoption of high performance working, SSDA Catalyst, issue 3.

* Hackman, J.R. and Oldham, G.R., 1980. Work redesign. Reading, MA: Addison Wesley.

* Hakanen, J., Bakker, A.B. and Schaufeli, W.B., 2006. Burnout and work engagement among teachers. The Journal of School Psychology, 43, pp. 495-513.

* Hallam G.L., 1996. The adventures of team fantastic: a practical guide for team leaders and members. [e-book] Greensboro, N.C.: Center for Creative Leadership. Available through: ASB Library website <http://www.asb.eblib.com. ez.statsbiblioteket.dk> [Accessed 20 May 2012 at 22:12 hrs)].

* Hallberg U.E. and Schaufeli W.B., 2006. "Same same" but different? Can work engagement be discriminated from job involvement and organizational commitment?.European Psychologist, 11(2), pp. 119–27.

* Harter, J.K., Schmidt, F.L. and Hayes, T.L., 2002. Business-unit-level relationship between employee satisfaction, employee engagement, and business outcomes: A meta-analysis. Journal of Applied Psychology, 87, pp.268-279.

* Heintzman R. and Marson B., 2005. Employees, service and trust: Links in a public sector service value chain. International Review of Administrative Studies, 7(4), pp. 549-575.

* Heintzman, Ralph, and Brian Marson, 2005, 'Employees, service and trust: is there a public sector service value

chain?' International Review of Administrative Sciences, 71, no 4, pp 549-575

❖ Hermsen, J. and Rosser, V., 2008. Examining Work Engagement and Job Satisfaction of Staff Members in Higher Education. CUPA-HR Journal. 59(2), pp. 10-18.

❖ hindalco.com, Wikipedia, money control (Accessed on 16th Jun 2014 at 23:30 hrs)

❖ HR managers Interview, http://smallbusiness.chron.com/interview-questions-human-resource-managers-1156.html (Accessed on 12th May 2014 at 22:00 hrs)

❖ Huang, J &Tansley, C (2012), Sneaking through the minefield of talent management : The notion of rhetorical obfuscation. International Journal of Human Resource Management, 23(17), 3673-3691.

❖ http://en.wikipedia.org/wiki/Manufacturing (Accessed on 11th Jun 2014 at 23:30 hrs)

❖ http://en.wikipedia.org/wiki/Organizational_culture(Accessed on 15th Jun 2014 at 23:30 hrs)

❖ http://in.mt.com/in/en/home.html(Accessed on 15th Jun 2014 at 23:30 hrs)

❖ http://nothingbuthoopla.com/2014/04/27/w-for-well-being/(Accessed on 15th Jun 2014 at 21:00 hrs)

❖ http://nwia.idwellness.org/2011/02/28/definitions-of-wellbeing-quality-of-life-and-wellness/#sthash.spqaswsS.dpuf (Accessed on 20th Jun 2014, at 22:00 hrs)

❖ http://opin.ca/article/engaged-vs-disengaged-employees#sthash.ZzkoBeTi.dpuf (Accessed on 12th Jun 2014 at 23:30 hrs)

❖ http://www.answers.com/topic/balasore-alloys-limited (Accessed on 19th Jun 2014 at 22:30 hrs)

❖ http://www.artofthestart.com/importance-of-training/ (Accessed on 12th Jun 2014 at 23:30 hrs)

* http://www.employersforwork-lifebalance.org.uk/how-does-work-life-balance-affect-employee-engagement/ (Accessed on 13th Jun 2014 at 22:30 hrs)

* http://www.genus.in (Accessed on 15th Jun 2014 at 23:30 hrs)

* http://www.godrejandboyce.com/(Accessed on 15th Jun 2014 at 23:30 hrs)

* http://www.nbrii.com/pdf/employee/Engaged_or_Disengaged.pdf(Accessed on 14th Jun 2014 at 23:30 hrs)

* https://wikispaces.psu.edu/display/PSYCH484/11.+Job+Satisfaction#id-11.JobSatisfaction-TheImportanceofJobSatisfactiontoEmployeeRetention (Accessed on 18th Jun 2014 at 23:00 hrs)

* (http://www.cisco.com/web/IN/about/network/manufacturing.html) (Accessed on 15th Jun 2014 at 23:30 hrs)

* http://www.yourhrworld.com/formats/search/hrorganizationstructure/(Accessed on 31st Jan 2014 at 21:00 hrs)

* Igbaria, M. and Buimaraes, T., 1993. Antecedents and consequences of job satisfaction among information center employees. Journal of Management Information Systems, 9(4), pp.145–175.

* IIes, P, Precece, D, &Chuai, X (2010). Talent management as a management fashion in HRD : Towards a research agenda. Human Resource Development International, 13(2), 125-145.

* Importance of employee engagement in business environment; http://pure.au.dk/portalasbstudent/files/45628761/Employee_Engagement.pdf, (Accessed on 01 Feb 2014 at 22:00 hrs)

* Indian Brand Equity Foundation; http://www.ibef.org/industry/manufacturingsectorindia. (Accessed on 12th March 2014 at 23:00 hrs)

- Information Systems Administrator Advisory Board Meeting; http://web.bpcc.edu/tem/accreditation/atmae2013/documents/appendixd71.pdf (Accessed on 25th Oct 2013)

- Inkson, K (2008). Are humans resources ? Career Development International, 13(3), 270-279

- ISSN: 0021-9010

- Jay B Barney, Organisational culture : can it be a source of sustained competitive advantage, Academy of Management Review, 1990, vol IICharles A O'Reilly III; Jennifer Chatman; David F Caldwell, Employees and Organisational culture: A profile comparison approach to assessing person organisation fit; The Academy of Management Journal, vol 34, issue 3 (Sep 1991)

- John T Delaney, Mark A Huselid, The impact of human resources management practices on perceptions of organisational performance; Academy of Management Journal, 1996, Vol 39, No 4, 949-969

- Johnsrud, L.K. and Rosser, V.J., 1999. College and University Midlevel Administrators: Explaining and Improving Their Morale. The Review of Higher Education, 22(2), pp. 121-141.

- Jump up^ Minchington, B (2006) Your Employer Brand – attract, engage, retain, Collective Learning Australia.

- Jurkiewicz, C. and Brown, R.,1998. GenXer's vs. boomers vs. matures: generational comparisons of public employees' motivation. Review of Public Personnel Administration, 18(4), pp.18–37.

- Kahn, W., 1990. Psychological conditions of personal engagement and disengagement at work. Academy of Management Journal, 33, pp. 692-724.

- Kahn, W., 1992. To be full there: psychological presence at work. Human Relations, 45, pp. 321-49.

- Kanuk and Berenson, Mail surveys, p.450 Reprinted from the Journal of Marketing Research, published by the American Marketing Association, in B. Blumberg, D.R. Cooper, P.S.

Schindler, 2005. Business research methods. London: McGraw-Hill.

❖ Karsan. R., 2011. Engaging and aligning employees. Training Journal, p.52-55

❖ Kathryn M. Page Æ Dianne A. Vella-Brodrick Accepted: 27 May 2008/Published online: 1 July 2008

❖ Koyuncu, M., Burke, R.J. and Fiksenbaum, L., 2006. Work engagement among womenmanagers and professionals in a Turkish bank: potential antecedents and consequences. Equal Opportunities International, 25, pp. 299-310.

❖ Kristin Backhaus, Surinder Tikoo, (2004) "Conceptualizing and researching employer branding", Career Development International, Vol. 9 Iss: 5, pp.501-517

❖ Kristof, A.L.,1996. Person–Organization Fit: An Integrative Review of Its Conceptualizations, Measurement, and Implications. Personnel Psychology, 49 (1), pp. 1–49.

❖ Langelaan, S., Bakker, A.B., Schaufeli, W.B., Van Rhenen, W. and Van Doornen, L.J.P., 2006. Do burned-out and work-engaged employees differ in the functioning of 62

❖ Lawler, E.E. and Hall, D.T., 1970. Relationship of job characteristics to job involvement, satisfaction, and intrinsic motivation. Journal of Applied Psychology, 54, pp. 305–312.

❖ Lockwood, N.R., 2007 Leveraging Employee Engagement for Competitive

❖ Lockwood, N.R., 2007. Leveraging Employee Engagement for Competitive Advantage: HR's Strategic Role. HR Magazine, 52(3), Special section pp. 1-11.

❖ Luthans, F., Avey, J.B., Avolio, B.J., Norman, S.M. and Combs, G.M., 2006. Psychological capital development: Toward a micro-intervention. Journal of Organizational Behavior, 27, pp. 387–393.

❖ Lweis, R & Heckman, R (2006). Talent Management : A critical review. Human Resource Management Review, 16(2), 139-154.

❖ Mamta, Sharma R. Baldev(2011), "Study of Employee Engagement and its Predictors in an Indian Public Sector Undertaking".

❖ Marisa Salanova and Sonia Agut, "Linking Organizational Resources and Work Engagement to Employee Performance and Customer Loyalty: The Mediation of Service Climate". Journal of Applied Psychology 2005, Vol. 90, No. 6, 1217–1227

❖ Markos, S. and Sridevi M.S., 2010. Employee Engagement: The Key to Improving Performance. International Journal of Business and Management, 5(12), pp. 89-96.

❖ Markos, S., & Sridevi, M.S. (2010). Employee engagement: The key to improving performance. International Journal of Business and Management, 5(12), 89-96.

❖ Maslach, C., Schaufeli, W.B. and Leiter, M.P., 2001. Job burnout. Annual Review of Psychology, 52, pp. 397-422.

❖ Mauno S., Kinnunen U. and Ruokolainen M., 2007. Job demands and resources as antecedents of work engagement: a longitudinal study. Journal of Vocational Behavior, 70, pp. 149–171.

❖ May, D.R., Gilson, R.L. and Harter, L.M., 2004. The psychological conditions of meaningfulness, safety, and availability and the engagement of the human spirit at work. Journal of Occupational Psychology, 77, pp. 11-37.

❖ 'Meaning at work research report' by Penna (2006) (http://www.penna.com/contentfiles/penna/content/research/e7031f6c-e95e-49ba-9ecc-fad74a0829ec/meaning_at_work.pdf) (Accessed on 15th Jun 2014 at 23:30 hrs)

❖ Minchington, B (2010) Employer Brand Leadership – A Global Perspective, Collective Learning Australia.

❖ Mone, E.M., and London, M., 2010. Employee Engagement: Through Effective Performance Management – A Practical Guide for Managers. Taylor & Francis Group NY.

* Ms. J.Josephine Virginia Sharmila, Employee engagement - an approach to organisational excellence, International Journal of Social Science & Interdisciplinary Research ISSN 2277 3630 IJSSIR, Vol. 2 (5), MAY (2013)

* N Venkataraman; Vasudevan Ramanujam; The Academy of Management Review, Vol 11,issue 4(Oct 1986) 801-814

* Nelson, D.L., Macik-Frey, M. and Quick, J.C., 2007. Advances in Occupational Health: From a Stressful Beginning to a Positive Future. Journal of Management, 33(6), pp. 809-840

* Ologbo, C.A. and Saudah, S., 2011. Engaging Employees who Drive Execution and Organizational Performance. American Journal of Economics and Business Administration, 3(3), pp. 569-575.

* Paradise, A., 2008. Influences Engagement. T+D, 62(1), pp. 54-59.

* Penna, 2006. Meaning at Work Research Report. Available at: <http://www.e-penna.com/newsopinion/research.aspx> [Accessed 28 March 2012].

* Porter, C., 2008. Exploring human resource management. London: McGaw-Hill p.442

* Practicum in Human Services Online Course Introduction http://cte.sfasu.edu/course/practicumin humanservicesonlinecourse/(Accessed on 20th March 2013, at 20:50 hrs)

* Psychological Well-being: Evidence Regarding its

* Punia B. K & Sharma Priyanka (2008) Employees Perspective on Human Resource Procurement Practices as Retention Tool in Indian IT Sector. Journal of Organizational, Vol. 12, Issue 4, pp.57-69.

* Quick, J.C., Macik-Frey, M. and Cooper, C.L., 2007. Managerial Dimensions of Organizational Health: The Healthy Leader at Work. Journal of Management Studies, 44(2), pp. 189 – 205.

❖ Rashid, H.A., Asad, A. and Ashraf, M.M., 2011. Factors Persuading Employee Engagement and Linkage of EE to Personal & Organizational Performance. Interdisciplinary Journal of Contemporary Research in Business, 3(5), pp. 98-108.

❖ Research report city of london corporation March 2014

❖ Rhoades,.L, Eisenberger, R. and Armeli, S., 2001. Affective commitment to the organization: the contribution of perceived organizational support. Journal of Applied Psychology, 86, pp. 825-36. 63

❖ Rhoades, L. and Eisenberger, R. 2002. Perceived organizational support: a review of the literature. Journal of Applied Psychology, 87, pp. 698-714.

❖ Richard, S. W. Audrey, B. S. & Scott E, (2011). Nine best practices for effective talent management. Development Dimensions International Inc. White paper available online www.aberdeen.com.

❖ RIGHT JOB ATTITUDE LEADS TO JOB SATISFACTION, http://rierc.org/social/paper292.pdf, (Accessed on 23rd Jul 2013, at 00:15 hrs)

❖ Robertson-Smith G. and Markwick C., 2009. Employee Engagement A review of current thinking. Institute for Employment Studies, Report 469.

❖ Robinson, D., 2007. Engagement is marriage of various factors at work. Thought Leaders, pp.37.

❖ Robinson, D., Perryman, S. and Hayday, S., 2004. The Drivers of Employee Engagement. Institute for Employment Studies, Brighton

❖ Role of employee engagement in building job satisfaction among employees of automotive industries in india c. swarnalatha & g. sureshkrishna, (ijhrmr)ISSN 2249-6874Vol. 3, Issue 1, Mar 2013,

❖ Rosser V.J., 2000. Midlevel Administrators: What We Know. New Directions for Higher Education, 111, pp. 5-13.

❖ Sakari Taipale, Kirsikka Selander, Timo Anttila, Jouko Nätti (2011)

❖ Saks, A.M., 2006. Antecedents and consequences of employee engagement. Journal of Managerial Psychology, 21, pp, 600-619.

❖ Salanova, M., Agut, S. and Peiro, J.M., 2005. Linking organizational resources and work engagement to employee performance and customer loyalty: the mediation of service climate. Journal of Applied Psychology, 90(6), pp. 1217–1227.

❖ Salanova, M., Llorens, S., Cifre, E., Martı´nez, I. and Schaufeli, W.B., 2003. Perceived collective efficacy, subjective well-being and task performance among electronic work groups: An experimental study. Small Groups Research, 34, pp. 43–73.

❖ Sanchez, P. and McCauley, D. 2006. Measuring and Managing Engagement in a Cross-Cultural Workforce: New Insights for Global Organisations. Global Business and Organizational Excellence, 26(1), pp. 41 – 50.

❖ Sange, R. & Srivasatava R.K., 2012. Employee Engagement and Mentoring: An Empirical Study of Sales Professionals. Synergy, 10(1), pp. 37-50

❖ Schaufeli and Salanova, 2007) Schaufeli, W.B. and Salanova, M., 2007. Work engagement: an emerging psychological concept and its implications for organizations. In: S.W. Gilliland, D.D. Steiner, and D.P. Skarlicki, ed, 2007, Research in Social Issues in Management: Managing Social and Ethical Issues in Organizations, Information Age Publishers, Greenwich, CT

❖ Schaufeli, W., Martı´nez, I., Marque´s-Pinto, A., Salanova, M. and Bakker, A.B., 2002. Burnout and engagement in university students: A crossnationa study. Journal of Cross-Cultural Psychology, 33, pp. 464–481.

❖ Schaufeli, W.B. and Bakker, A.B., 2004. Job demands, job resources and their relationship with burnout and engagement: a multisample study. Journal of Organizational Behavior, 25, pp. 293–315.

❖ Schaufeli, W.B. and Salanova, M., 2007. Work engagement: an emerging psychological concept and its implications for organizations. In: S.W. Gilliland, D.D. Steiner, and D.P. Skarlicki, ed, 2007, Research in Social Issues in Management: Managing Social and Ethical Issues in Organizations, Information Age Publishers, Greenwich, CT.

❖ Schaufeli, W.B., Bakker, A.B. and Van Rhenen, W., 2009. How changes in job demands and resources predict burnout, work engagement, and sickness absenteeism. Journal of Organizational Behavior, 30(7), pp. 893 – 917.

❖ Schaufeli, W.B., Salanova, M., Gonzalez-Roma, V. and Bakker, A.B., 2002. The measurement of engagement and burnout: A two sample organisatio national factor analytic approach. Journal of Happiness Studies, 3, pp. 71-92.

❖ Schon& Ian, (2009) : The global "war for talent"; Journal of International Management 15 (2009), 273-285.

❖ Schneider, B. & Bowen, D., 1993. The service organization: Human resource management is crucial. Organizational Dynamics, 21, pp. 39–52.

❖ Scott, R.A., 1978. Lords, Squires and Yeoman: Collegiate Middle Managers and Their Organizations. Washington, D.C.: American Association for Higher Education. 64

❖ Scottish Executive, 2007. Employee engagement in the Public Sector: a review of literature. Available at: <http://www.scotland.gov.uk/Publications/2007/05/09111348/3> [Accessed 27 March 2012, at 22:45 hrs].

❖ Seijts, G.H. and Crim, D., 2006. What engages employees the most or, the ten C's of employee engagement. Ivey Business Journal Online, 70(4), pp. 1-5.

❖ Shamir, B., House, R.J. and Arthur, M.B., 1993. The motivational effect of charismatic leadership: A self-concept based theory. Organization Science, 4, pp. 577–594.

❖ Sharma Baldev R et al (2010 Sharma, Baldev. R et al (2010) Determinants of Employee Engagement in a Private Sector Organization: An Exploratory Study, Advances in Management, Vol. 3, Issue 10, pp.52-59.

❖ Sharma Baldev R et al (2010 Sharma, Baldev. R et al (2010) Determinants of Employee Engagement in a Private Sector Organization: An Exploratory Study, Advances in Management, Vol. 3, Issue 10, pp.52-59.

❖ Shuck, B. and Wollard, K., 2010. Employee Engagement and HRD: A Seminal Review of the Foundations Human Resource Development Review, 9(1), pp. 89-110.

❖ Shuck, B., 2011. Four Emerging Perspectives of Employee Engagement: An Integrative Literature Review. Human Resource Development Review, 10(3), pp. 304-328.

❖ Shuck, M Brad; Rocco, Tonette S; Albornoz, Carlos A.Exploring employee engagement from the employee perspective: implications for HRD. Journal of European Industrial Training 35.4 (2011): 300-325.

❖ Song, J.H. and Kim, H.M., 2009. The integrative structure of employee commitment: The influential relations of individuals' characteristics in a supportive learning culture. Leadership and Organization Development Journal, 30(3), pp.240–255.

❖ Song, J.H., Kolb, J.A., Lee, U.H. and Kim, H.K., 2012. Role of transformational leadership in effective organizational knowledge creation practices: Mediating effects of employees' work engagement. Human Resource Development Quarterly, 23(1), pp. 65-101.

❖ Sonnentag (2003) Recovery, work engagement, and proactive behavior: A new look at the interface between nonwork and work, Journal of Applied Psychology, 2003, 88 (3), 518-528, 67 Literaturang.

❖ Sonnentag, S., 2003. Recovery, work engagement, and proactive behaviour: a new look at the interface between non-work and work. Journal of Applied Psychology, 88(3), pp. 518–528.

❖ Subjective Well-Being: An Intersection between Economics and Psychology By Christopher J. Boyce Thesis submitted in fulfilment of the requirements for the degree of Doctor of Philosophy in Psychology University of Warwick, Department of Psychology September 2009

❖ Subjective Well-Being: An Intersection between Economics and Psychology; http://www2.warwick.ac.uk/alumni/ services/eportfolios/psrfbb/chris_boyce_thesis_-_corrected. pdf/(Accessed on 29th Jun 2014, at 21: 24 hrs)

❖ Sy, T., Cote, S. and Saavedra, R., 2005. The contagious leader: impact of leader's affect on group member affect and group processes. Journal of Applied Psychology, 90, pp. 295-305.

❖ Talent Management is as Critical as Capital Investment : Dr Vipul Saxena & Dr RK Srivastava - International Journal of Business Management & Research (IJBMR); ISSN (P): 2249-6920; ISSN (E): 2249-8036 ; Vol. 8, Issue 4, Aug 2018, 27-32

❖ Temkin, B., 2012. Employee Engagement Benchmark Study. Temkin Group. Available att: <http://experiencematters. wordpress.com/2012/02/02/small-organisations-have-more-engaged-employees/> [Accessed 25 May 2012 at 23:10 hrs].

❖ The 'What', 'Why' and 'How' of Employee Well-Being: A New Model, http://eric.ed.gov/?id=EJ818579 (Accessed on 29th Sep 2014 at 20:45 hrs)

❖ The Employment Value Proposition. Article which introduces the original concept, by Tandehill Human Capital. *Workspan*

Magazine 10/06 http://www.tandehill.com/pdfs/Total-Rewards.pdf (Accessed on 15th Jun 2014 at 23:30 hrs)

❖ The Essentials of Employee Engagement in Organizations Author: Simon, Simeon S 2011)

❖ "The four intrinsic rewards that drive employee engagement", by Kenneth Thomas, Vol.Nov/Dec 2009 p1& 2

❖ The hypothalamic-pituitary-adrenal axis?. Scandinavian Journal of Work, Environment, and Health, 32, pp. 339-48.

❖ The Influence of Rewards and Job Satisfaction on Employees in the Service Industry Author: Sarwar, Shagufta; Abugre, James

❖ Thiagarajan B & Renugadevi V (2011), Thiagarajan, B & Renugadevi, V (2011) Employee Engagement Practices in Indian BPO Industries-An Empirical Investigation. Interdisciplinary Journal of Contemporary Research in Business, Vol.2, Issue 10, pp.134-141

❖ Tims, M., Bakker, A.B., Xanthopoulou, D., 2011. Do transformational leaders enhance their followers' daily work engagement?. Leadership Quarterly, 22(1), pp. 121-131.

❖ Tobias Schlager, Mareike Bodderas, Peter Maas, Joël Luc Cachelin, (2011) "The influence of the employer brand on employee attitudes relevant for service branding: an empirical investigation", Journal of Services Marketing, Vol. 25 Iss: 7, pp.497-508

❖ Towers Perrin, 2003. Working today: understanding what drives employee engagement. Towers Perrin. Available at: <http://www.towersperrin.com/tp/getwebcachedoc?webc=HRS/USA/2003/200309/Talent_2003.pdf> [Accessed 6 March 2012, at 22: 00 hrs].

❖ Ulrika E. Hallberg, Gunnn Johansson Wilmar B. Schauffli "Type A behavior and work situation: Associations with burnout and work engagement", Scandinavian Journal of Psychology, 2007, 48, 135–142,

- Victor Bart et al (2000), Victor et al (2000) The effective design of work under total quality management. Organization science, Vol-11, pp.1.

- Wah, L., 1999. Engaging employees a big challenge. Management Review, 88(9), pp. 10. Well-being Institute, University of Cambridge, UK

- Westbrook, S. D., 1980. Morale Proficiency and Discipline. Journal of Political and Military Sociology, 8(1), pp. 43 – 54.

- Westman, M., 2001. Stress and strain crossover. Human Relations, 54, pp. 557-91.

- Work engagement in eight European countries: The role of job demands, autonomy, and social support

- www.ahlstrom.com(Accessed on 15th Jun 2014 at 23:30 hrs)

- www.kirloskar.com(Accessed on 19th Jun 2014 at 22:30 hrs)

- www.lawrenceandmayo.co.in (Accessed on 19th Jun 2014 at 22:30 hrs)

- www.mangroup.com(Accessed on 19th Jun 2014 at 22:30 hrs)

- www.motherson.com(Accessed on 19th Jun 2014 at 22:30 hrs)

- www.parikhindustries.com/(Accessed on 19th Jun 2014 at 22:30 hrs)

- www.pcblltd.com(Accessed on 19th Jun 2014 at 22:30 hrs)

- www.shyamgroup.com (Accessed on 19th Jun 2014 at 22:30 hrs)

- www.somaiya.com(Accessed on 19th Jun 2014 at 22:30 hrs)

- Xanthopoulou, D., Bakker, A.B., Demerouti, E. and Schaufeli, W.B., 2007. The role of personal resources in the job demands-resources model. International Journal of Stress Management, 14(2), pp. 121-41.